D1486638

JUN 16 2015

WITHDRAWN

JUN 2 6 2024

DAVID O. McKAY LIBRARY
BYU-IDAHO

3 1404 0080
AY LIBRARY

THE MIGHTY CHANGE

THE MIGHTY CHANGE

elaine cannon & ed j. pinegar

Deseret Book
Company
Salt Lake City,
Utah
1977

© 1977 by Deseret Book Company
All rights reserved
Printed in the United States of America
ISBN 0-87747-655-1

Library of Congress Cataloging in Publication Data

Cannon, Elaine.
    The mighty change.

    Includes index.
    1. Christian life—Mormon authors.   I. Pinegar,
Ed J., joint author.   II. Title.
BV4501.2.C263   248'.48'93   77-24708
ISBN 0-87747-655-1

And now behold,
I ask of you, my brethren
of the church, have ye
spiritually been born of God?
Have ye received his image
in your countenances?
Have ye experienced
this mighty change
in your hearts?

—Alma 5:14

To King Benjamin,
from whom we gleaned the six principles of change,
and to Alma the younger,
from whom we learned that all of us may experience the mighty
change by experimenting upon the Word and then in
turn helping others to progress spiritually

Contents

WHAT IF . . . ?

What if we lived in communities where we could walk in our parks in safety, sleep without bolting our doors, park without locking the car, and leave a ten-speed bicycle leaning against a porch piled high with the daily papers and then find everything in order when we return from vacation?

In such a community there would be no cheating at school, on income tax returns, or in business dealings. Business would flourish in fair trade, and everyone would prosper from a harvest handled by eager labor.

There would be no envy, no begrudging, no selfishness. The people would have all things in common.

There would be no lying nor tumult, no war nor contention. There would be no drunkenness, lasciviousness, pornography, robbery, rape, assault, nor murder.

No one would hate, scoff, scheme, quarrel, or complain. People would listen to each other. Their yearnings would be met, aching longings would be fulfilled, secrets kept, and broken hearts healed. Truth would be treasured and gossip avoided altogether.

People would lift up the hands that hang down, strengthen the feeble knees, carry each other's burdens, and forgive and forget. No one would suffer hurt feelings or self-pity.

In this place husbands and wives would love each other deeply and always. Children would learn only the good things, the tender, thoughtful, and delightful things from their parents. They would honor, obey, and love their parents. Everyone would enter upon the adventure of life wholeheartedly with an attitude of, "What good thing can I do for my family, my community, my fellowmen?" There would be no broken homes.

The people would pray to a God that they know lives, one who, they are certain, knows they live. In his name miracles would be performed, so that the blind could see, the deaf hear, and the lame walk swiftly, even run, on strong legs. Each sinner would repent and find peace until there would be no sin.

What if—oh, what if?

Most of us struggle to find a single moment of tranquillity, let alone a lifetime of it. Let us consider a comparison between two families.

The families live across the street from each other. The only visible difference between them is the number of children they have and what they do on Sunday. Members of one family pile into their camper and boat, laughing and waving their goodbyes. Members of the other family push and hurry their way into the over-crowded family car and scowl or sulk all the way to church.

This goes on for years until one of the children in the second family asks, "Why is going to church better than going boating if the Martins are happy and we're not?"

Why, indeed?

Well, father, who is supposed to give the opening prayer, shouts the alarm above the blaring television that the family van is leaving for church in five minutes and everyone had better be ready if they know where their peanut butter comes from. Older daughter is upset when she goes to put on her new blouse and finds younger sister already wearing it. Big brothers stir up a familiar storm playing keep-away with little brother's shoe. Big sister's hair won't curl right, and Merry Miss forgets to wash her face. Mom's nylon stocking has a run, and she has to hurry back into the bedroom to change. The baby is screaming, and Dad booms the minute-hand readings like an irritated referee. And no one smiles on his way to worship God!

To live in a "what if" family or community is not out of the realm of possibility for any of us. It need not be just a sweet dream. We can live after the manner of supreme happiness here on earth. There is a precedent for it. It is a remarkable but true story. It is about people who would be great to live next door to and to emulate.

The people in this community all repented of their sins, were baptized in the name of Christ, and received the Holy Ghost. They didn't just have hands placed upon their heads for the bestowal of the gift of the Holy Ghost, for the text says they "did *receive* the Holy Ghost." And so they dealt justly with one another in every way and were all "partakers of the heavenly gift." They knew joy and did marvelous works. They had all things in common.

Their lifestyle brought them peace, not frustration. They became increasingly attractive, delightsome, and fair. They were blessed in their marriages according to the multitude of promises the Lord had made to them. They built great cities and prospered exceedingly upon all the face of the land.

Others wanted to be like them and tried. Finally, "all the people in all the lands round about" followed their example. Both Nephite and Lamanite people—long-time traditional enemies—were soon living in peace with one another! The details of their highly successful civilization, which lasted for several generations, can be found in the book of 4 Nephi.

How did they do it? They were, according to the record, converted unto the Lord. Everyone. And it was wonderful.

The obvious thought that follows is that if we want to live in such a blissful state here on earth, we too need to become converted. With all the advantages of the gospel that are ours, we ought to be able to do so.

This doesn't mean we'll be spared disease, anxiety, grief, separation from our loved ones, or even that we will loll about in idleness. The rain falls on the just and the unjust. But when we are on the Lord's side, we can take what happens and grow from it. The gospel teaches us the will of God for us and the purpose of this earth. We are here to be tried, to overcome, to make choices, and to find our way back to Heavenly Father. The way is hard. But remember, no precious stone was ever cut into fabulous facets by a marshmallow. We live in the world, but we must keep trying not to be of the world. We may not be able to eliminate singlehandedly the crime and sin of the world, but we can feel good toward all mankind while we work toward becoming "what if" kinds of people.

We may not change society in one generation, but we can change ourselves. Then we can work on our families, moving forward steadily, coping with challenges. And we will be filled.

So, why not change?

CERTAIN KINDS OF PEOPLE

Why aren't we living in an ideal world with near-perfect people? Why aren't we more Christlike? The gospel has been restored. All the opportunities are here. So why not?

There are three types of people in the world: the rebellious, the righteous, and, hovering somewhere in between, those whom we might label as the receptive. Let's look at each of these groups.

Rebellious people are those who either have never heard the gospel of Jesus Christ or have not understood it. They are confused. They haven't cultivated the still small voice. They don't pray because they don't know to whom they should pray. They steal, cheat, hurt, commit crimes, and practice all manner of immoralities.

The world is full of rebellious, mixed-up people who willfully or unknowingly go against the will of God. Newspapers and other forms of mass media keep us informed of their abominable antics daily. We can only pity them, and then strengthen our resolve to spread the gospel into more corners more effectively.

Receptive people are receptive to the gospel teachings, the fine examples, the firm directives, and the lofty promises, but their actions lag behind. Most of us fall into this category. We know the difference between right and wrong. We have an idea about heaven. We may even be aware in a vague way of what it takes, finally, to become exalted. It's just that it is so far away—and we have a meeting to go to today.

Receptive people are merely convinced that the gospel is true. To them, however, it is really more of a fine social experience. It's smart to be anxiously engaged in good causes. A person stays out of a lot of trouble that way, and besides, it's good for the kids.

So a receptive person thinks nice thoughts, but often his heart falters and his will flags. He has been taught there is a God "up there somewhere." He prays to him in public, sometimes echoing the words of others, sometimes by rote, but he does pray. In times of crisis, he may pray in private. He wouldn't break the Ten Commandments in a clinical sense. That is, he wouldn't commit murder—but he might drive as if he were the only one on the road with any right of way. He wouldn't commit adultery—but if he finds a copy of a girlie magazine lying around, he might sneak a peak. He is well-meaning and he thinks the principles of the gospel are fine. He even thinks he is living them fully. After all, he has a temple recommend.

The *righteous person,* on the other hand, is one who is truly converted to Christ. He has deliberately made an effort to know God, to know all the gospel principles and apply them to his whole life. And it is changing him. He is experiencing the mighty change of which Alma speaks:

" . . . have ye spiritually been born of God? Have ye received his image in your countenances? Have ye experienced this mighty change in your hearts?

" . . . and a mighty change was . . . wrought in their hearts, and they humbled themselves and put their trust in the true and living God. And behold, they were faithful until the end; therefore they were saved." (Alma 5:14, 13.)

The righteous person has put his foot on the path toward

perfection. Through study and prayer and the witnessing power of the Holy Ghost, he has come to know God the Father and his Son Jesus Christ. He has confidence in their will. He knows they never ask us to abstain from anything that is good for us. Their way has been proven over and over again to be the best way—the only way.

The righteous person knows that the gospel is true and that it works. He has come to love the Lord so much that he wants to keep his commandments more than he wants to do anything else. He prays fervently, frequently, and in faith, out of a full heart. He prays in thanksgiving as well as in need, in private as well as in public. He prays for others. He prays for mercy and for strength to be what he knows he ought to be—and now wants to be. It hasn't anything much to do with what position he holds in church, but everything to do with how he feels inside about God, about himself, and about others. (See Alma 34:18-27.)

The righteous person lives a law higher than the law of Moses. He tries to live by all the laws of Jesus and his counsel given to us through living prophets today. He doesn't commit adultery and he doesn't sneak peaks at pornography. For him, this kind of temptation just doesn't exist. He works hard at keeping disturbing influences out of this life.

When it comes to personality problems, the righteous person refuses to show favor only to those who are friendly to him, such as the person who throws a business deal his way, or the one who is in complete agreement with his views during a committee meeting. Instead, like Alma and Nephi, who prayed earnestly for all their brethren, he feels deep love for others. As he grows, his love expands to include all mankind. He is compassionate with the confused or rebellious soul, the sinner, the enemy, the nagging neighbor, the auto mechanic who may cheat him a little, and his own mate, who has little faults that may annoy him.

The righteous person is a converted person. Being converted unto the Lord makes all the difference in one's life. A converted person tries to keep all the Lord's commandments all the time. He is in the process of being born again—or he may have made that transition already. We see it in his face and demeanor. We recognize it and marvel at it in his life. We love being around him because it is so nice, peaceful, and comfortable.

We feel closer to God, somehow, in the company of the righteous person, and this spurs us on in our own efforts to become like Christ. And perhaps this is an important clue. The truly righteous person does not offend us with a holier-than-thou attitude. He can't. He doesn't feel that way. He is humble. He knows Jesus and knows how far we all have to go to meet him. He is Christ's servant, busily trying to love and to lift others, when they are ready, into the same state of joy. He is a happy person.

What a tragedy it would be for us if we didn't become converted! What if we were merely convinced, passive members of the Church and never became righteous enough to qualify for life in the presence of God? What if . . . ?

Fortunately, Heavenly Father wants each of us back in his presence. He is not interested in losing any of us. Jesus came to earth to bring to pass the immortality and eternal life of man. It is a gift for us to take. The system set up by God to guide us in this pursuit is the gospel. This really is our advantage over the rest of the world. We have principles and policies, programs, priesthood ordinances, and prophets. We have special problems and disciplines that help in their own way as well.

Alma asked the people in ancient America if they had experienced the mighty change of heart. In Alma 5:13 he reminded them that their fathers had had the mighty change "wrought in their hearts, and they humbled themselves and put their trust in the true and living God . . . and they were faithful until the end; therefore they were saved."

But even before they were saved, these people lived stripped of envy, and they sang the song of redeeming love. They walked blameless before God and were thus prepared to meet him.

Perhaps we should ask ourselves Alma's questions. Have we experienced the mighty change of heart? Have we been spiritually born of God? Have we received his image in our countenance? The answers to these questions might explain why our communities fall so far short of the ideal. Certain kinds of people bring about certain kinds of communities.

SOMETHING TO THINK ABOUT

A dramatic painting of Christ's second coming hangs in the foyer of the Washington D.C. Temple. The artist has depicted Christ as a strikingly handsome, compelling figure. He seems to look directly into one's eyes. He is turned slightly, with his arms outstretched in welcome to those before him. Light radiates from his being and floods those who are kneeling at his feet and coming forth to be welcomed. They represent all generations, ranks, and activities of man. There are royalty and peasants, young and old, lame and whole, white and dark.

Behind the figure of Christ, in the shadows, are the same kinds of people. These persons, however, aren't kneeling. They were rebellious ones who are now writhing in agony and weeping. Those in the light were righteous and are being received by Christ. Those in the darkness are sorely disappointed not to have qualified before him.

This mural is a very effective representation of a basic truth of life: Each man earns his own reward, and the day of reckoning will surely come.

During the weeks before the temple was dedicated, the public was invited to tour it. Some of the personnel there became aware of the startling effect the magnificent mural had upon visitors. As the people in line walked slowly forward toward it, those ahead in the line seemed to blend right in with the people in the mural. And as the people in line pressed closer to the mural, an interesting thing often happened. They would shift, seemingly unconsciously, toward the left. They wanted to be in the light! The misery of the people in the dark was depressing, and the viewer often felt uncomfortable even standing near that dark side of the mural.

Christ's mission is to bring to pass the immortality and eternal life of man. Our mission is to accept this awesome gift and, through valiant self-effort, bring about the necessary growth toward perfection that will earn our exaltation. Unless we have examined ourselves recently and found perfection present, we surely have a need for change.

We are not like Christ yet, of course. But he has said that we can be like him. He has specifically told us, "What manner of men ought ye to be? Even as I am."

We should be concerned with becoming like him in all the ways we can. Perhaps his most distinguishing characteristic is his capacity for love. We aren't concerned with whether he is good at interior decoration, fishing, basketball, music, or science. Therefore, we ought to be more concerned about our own ability to love and be loved than some of the other pursuits we busy ourselves with.

When a bishop's interview, a priesthood message, or our own self-examination reveals that we aren't quite what we need to be in some area, we should take the necessary steps to change. If our hearts are warmed toward the Savior, we will want to hasten the change. We will give thanks for new insights and saving principles instead of feeling resentful or defensive about having our shortcomings exposed.

Assuming that we would like to make some personal progress, how do we begin such a sweeping, sweetening project? What do we change first?

Moroni 7 provides a special kind of yardstick by which we can measure our behavior, our decisions, and our choices. For example, those things that make us feel complacent or defensive or that lead us away from praying to Heavenly Father are the things we need to start changing first.

Sometimes we have a tendency to explain away our weaknesses by stubbornly saying, "Well, that's just how I am. I can't change." Or we hide our foolishness behind lies. Or we justify our actions by declaring we are deprived in other areas. Or we blame it on someone else, such as our parents. Or, forgetting that there are eternal laws irrevocably decreed, we may insist, "God is merciful. He knows my problems. He won't forsake me." And we go along with a kind of false security, a postponement of reality.

Before we can comfortably dwell in Christ's presence, we must be guiltless. We must radiate love. We must be perfect, even as he is perfect.

The only way true change can be brought about is to be willing to admit that we are imperfect in some important areas—in our capacity to love as Christ loves, for example. This seems to be a first step to the humble spirit and contrite heart that the Lord has said is necessary to open the way to his presence. He has also promised us that all things are possible through him. That's where our confidence to change comes from, as well as the directions for the effort. (See Philippians 4:13.)

What will mark our progress along the way? Self-control might be defined as doing what is best or appropriate for us more often than not. So, as we see ourselves growing more controlled, we notice increased opportunities for service. A sense of well-being fills us. We qualify for increased blessings and additional sacred ordinances. We can cope with the exigencies of life with a finer attitude and greater skill.

What we really need is a good understanding of the basic principles of life and those ordinances and powers that move us along toward perfection.

But wait! Before we become bored with this statement, insisting we've heard it all before, let us remember Alma's mission to the Zoramites and his attempts to reactivate them in the gospel. They had heard the word of God before too, but their lives were far from being spiritually oriented. (See Alma 31.)

This can happen to us. How many of us think we're righteous because we keep the Word of Wisdom? How many of us are positive we are living the gospel but still go about gossiping, divorcing, weeping and wailing, and breaking the Sabbath now and then? Do we know which of our Heavenly Father's basic principles will help us in which situations?

When we turn back to God, we find he has the answers. The Master knows the man, and His word is in the scriptures. The scriptures have been compiled by God's chosen prophets and servants down through the ages for the good of mankind. They are full of choice examples of man's experiences with God and in dealing with the rugged challenges of life. As we read about other members of God's family in the scriptures, we can learn important lessons that will help us in our own lives. We can become familiar with particular laws we must keep in order to reap particular blessings. All the laws, irrevocably decreed in heaven before this earth was created, by which even God is bound, and upon which all blessings are predicated (see D&C 130:20), are found in the scriptures.

We can also learn the will of the Lord for us and become closer to him through the power and gifts of the Holy Ghost. This is a beautiful blessing that we rarely take full advantage of. We seem almost surprised when we have an experience that proves the gift!

Each of us who is baptized a member of The Church of Jesus Christ of Latter-day Saints has hands placed upon his head by those holding authority from God to confirm him and to bestow the gift of the Holy Ghost. Then it is up to us to receive the Holy Ghost, to earnestly seek its influence so we can have its power to inspire us, to teach and enlighten us, to warn and comfort us, and to help us discern right from wrong, truth from error, good from evil. It is a witness to us of the reality of God and the validity of the mission of his Son Jesus Christ.

But we have to seek for the influence of the Holy Ghost continually. It is not forced upon us against our own agency. And it cannot operate in our lives if we are not clean, humble, and repentant.

A young missionary had been led, deliberately and carefully, into temptation by an investigator of the Church—and he did succumb. He was excommunicated and promptly sent home in disgrace. When he arrived, he fell into the arms of his loved ones and cried in mighty repentance, "Oh, why did I do it? Why? Why? And now the Spirit has left me. I know it. I can feel the emptiness. It is gone. Oh, it is gone. How will I manage now, if I couldn't before?"

In the touching moments that followed, a heartbroken father taught truth that he admitted he should have explained more carefully earlier. The bestowal of the gift doesn't necessarily mean that the individual receives it. A careful reading of the scriptures reveals this. The Holy Ghost may descend upon a man but not tarry with him. (D&C 130:23.) We need to be conscious of our weaknesses and cry out in faith for our need. If we set about with renewed vigor of purpose to keep the commandments the best we can, and enlist Heavenly Father's help, we will be blessed with an outpouring of the Spirit.

As we live ever closer to the Lord, we'll enjoy more gifts of the Holy Ghost.

The young missionary was bereft when he knew he was without the Spirit. It happened so fast in him that he could easily recall what it was like before, when he was pure. With most of us it is a case of withdrawing ourselves in little ways, slowly but surely short-circuiting the power of the Holy Ghost within us. Other things crowd in. Dissenting spirits take over. We lean upon the arm of flesh instead of the power of God. We think everything is fine until the gradual closing of our hearts, by choices along the way, leaves us in a poor position to make good judgments or resist temptation.

We are difficult to reach when we have let our hearts become hardened. The missionary was reachable. But to those of us who think we are righteous already, that we are living the gospel fully now, it may come as a jolt to consider that we really aren't Christlike when we can't live in love in our homes, work together in peace, discipline with patience, and endure sickness and disappointment with serenity and faith.

For example, a group of good friends were discussing a couple they knew well who had gone through divorce after many years of marriage and family life, responsible service in the Church, and exemplary positions in the community. It was a shock to everyone that this sort of thing could happen to "people like that," people who are supposed to know all the good answers and do all the wise things.

Someone said, "How could they dare get a divorce in this society?"

"What went wrong?" asked another person. "Could we have helped them?"

Then one member of the group quietly but firmly suggested that the couple probably hadn't been really living the gospel and it ought to be a lesson to all who were participating in the discussion.

"Hadn't been living the gospel?" exclaimed another in surprise. "What do you mean? Weren't they keeping the Word of Wisdom? They went to all their meetings. They served in the Church. What do you mean?"

The other person was thoughtful a moment and then explained, "It has to do with being converted. As I am coming to understand the gospel of Jesus Christ, living it means to be Christlike. It means one will give and forgive, be patient, tolerant, supportive, helpful, loyal, and loving. It isn't just not smoking or drinking. It is selflessness in private and public situations. We know these people. We've described their lifestyle. But have they, in fact, been publicly supportive and tender to each other in all the years we've known them? And have they cleaved only to each other through boredom and anxiety, through trial and through plenty? If they were being Christlike, wouldn't they put a fine example to their children and others ahead of self-interest?"

Everyone was silent a moment. It was the kind of incisive interpretation of the gospel that could make a difference in everyone's life. We know the things pertaining to qualifying for a temple recommend, but are we converted unto the Lord so that we echo his phrases of love to those around us? The Savior said that the Spirit giveth life. Are we giving life to our relationships?

People who are converted live by the Spirit. Their lives are as close to fullness and happiness as we can know on earth. They try to solve their problems by using the principles of the gospel and not the precepts of men found in an advice column or during a telephone conversation. Converted people lean upon God and they learn from him through the scriptures and the Spirit. This is the wise way our Heavenly Father has for us to live and grow with as little heartache as possible.

All of us would rather solve our problems beautifully than hazard our lives. But not all of us are yet prepared to do so. We are busy at something else or we've forgotten to tune in recently or we just don't know the gospel well enough or we aren't in the habit of living it to succeed as we should.

Alma knew this. After his experience with the Zoramites, he was greatly grieved, just as their friends were over the divorce of this prominent couple. Alma had gone to preach the word of God among the Zoramites in a way they could understand so that they would change their ways. He had taken his best missionaries with him after he had given them a blessing and the Spirit was with them. They were prepared. They were enthusiastic and conscientious. They tried everything. But the Zoramites would not listen. Their hearts were hard, and "they began to be offended because of the strictness of the word." (Alma 35:15.)

Have we been offended when a prophet has asked us to store supplies, to lengthen our stride, to not use face cards for entertainment, to make our marriages meaningful? Have we been offended when someone has suggested we weren't living the gospel as purely as we might? Have we felt a terrible twinge when forgiveness or patience or loving someone unappealing is required of us? When the topic of the sermon is "Unto the Least of These," are we offended at such hard requirements?

The Zoramites couldn't be helped because they would not be helped. Could this be true with divorced couples, wayward children, selfish singles, proud priesthood leaders, and martyr-mothers?

Life is difficult. It also can be full of joy. Commandments may seem too difficult or offensive to us unless we judge them by their fruits. They are to help us. It remains for us to be helped. Perhaps the big difference in heartaches, after all, is the way we face them. One person will finally feel stronger, through it all, if he has been guided, sustained, and comforted by the Lord and his principles. Another will harden his heart and become frustrated and embittered by trials. Divorce, disgrace, disenchantment, disappointment, tragedy through illness or accident might press in on all of us in time. As we keep growing closer to the Lord and his sweet, wise counsel, we can be ready for the advance of any new problem that may beset us.

It isn't just living the gospel and becoming Christlike so we can endure our trials, however. Surely there is power in people whose lives conform to Christ's. They can serve others much more effectively.

Alma did one more interesting, touching thing. He came back from his mission to the Zoramites—his brethren who had grown up in the same "ward"—and wondered if perhaps his own family really understood the gospel and what it meant to be like God. Once more he called them all together so he might give unto each one his counsel, separately, "concerning the things pertaining unto righteousness." (Alma 35:16.) Alma recorded the valuable instructions concerning the gospel that he gave his sons. They are found in chapters 36 through 42 of the book of Alma.

Perhaps we need to look again at where we are, what we know, and how we have progressed. Perhaps we should consider the state of those over whom we have stewardship, daring to evaluate our own Christlikeness and theirs, helping as we can.

Even though we might have gone through the Church system, served in positions, and kept certain of the commandments, unless we have been humble and open-hearted we might not have received the truth unto our conversion. Alma had success with just a few of the Zoramites, and it was with those who were in a "state of preparedness" to receive the word. In Matthew 13 we learn of the parable of the sower describing the many threats to the seed or word of God. The soil has to be just so. The weeds of worldliness must not be allowed to choke it. So it is with us. Before we can receive the word of God unto our own benefit, we need to have hearts ready to receive it.

The mural in the Washington D.C. Temple gives us something to think about. Only a contrite heart, humility, and an ever-increasing attempt to become like Christ will put us in the light, on life's canvas.

THE ELEMENTS OF CHANGE

The Savior said, ". . . what manner of men ought ye to be? Verily I say unto you, even as I am." (3 Nephi 27:27.) And that leaves room for improvement in anyone's life.

Let us consider certain elements of change necessary to bring ourselves into a compatible state with the Savior.

Change in a human being is, of course, a continuing process. It is wrapped and bound with the first principles and ordinances of the restored gospel of Jesus Christ. The first principle is faith in Jesus Christ, the man and his mission, his role, and his authority as the Son of God.

The second principle is repentance or turning away from anything in our life that is anti-Christ and beginning to move in a direction that will take us back into his presence.

The first ordinance is submitting humbly to the immersion of our bodies in the waters of baptism. We bury our sins therein and emerge clean, with a new life.

The second ordinance is the gift of the Holy Ghost by the laying on of hands by those with authority to do so. From there we begin our true growth in understanding the eternal truths of the gospel and applying them to every aspect of our lives. We do not understand all truths at once. We, like the Savior, receive things line upon line, grace upon grace. Keeping this in mind should keep us from the depressing attitude of the "nobody's perfect, so why try?" syndrome.

Change is ever with us. If we don't move forward, we move backward. Our goal is to become born again of the Spirit, to become so like Christ that he is reflected in our countenance, and to deal with life as he would have us do. If we slip a step, we can repent and give thanks for the atonement of Christ and begin the path to godliness again.

Real enlightenment comes to the whole process when we awaken to the strength and power of the spirit that is within us. The spirit can direct the body. It can be a strong, lovely dictator of the body's actions, or it can be left uncultivated in the ways of God and be weak, disobedient, bitter, and, finally, ungodlike. The spirit relinquishes its chance to obey the Father unto the fullness of joy when it chooses the easy trail of the world. This is simply part of the premortal battle between the coercive approach of the adversary and the gentle approach of the Savior, which allows man choice and growth.

Guidance for any change must come at a person's level of understanding and ability to absorb. We mirror our environment in our actions. We tend to behave as we are taught by the examples and pressures in our lives unless a stronger force comes into play in our life, in which case the forces *for* change must be mobilized and given direction in order to resist the forces *against* change.

A Harvard Business School report on the matter of organizational change, prepared under the direction of Gene Dalton, stresses this point keenly. The observation is made that the same truth exists in bringing about change in an individual as in an organization. "The persons being influenced need confidence that change can be effected. A large part of this confidence comes initially from their faith in the power and judgment of the influencing agent. When men are unsure of their capacity to cope effectively with the situation, they identify with someone whom they perceive as having the knowledge or power to successfully cope with it and who states where they need to change. As such, he is then placed in a position where his expectations can become self-fulfilling prophecies."

In other words, people in need of change are likely to follow the believable one who gets to them first. Sometimes the world wins out over religion simply because it is heard so often, shouts the loudest, or has such clever authorities. One thing we know, worldliness is working mighty hard to win the troops!

We go to diet centers, psychiatrists, music teachers, school rooms, or private tutors for special instructions. We have confidence they can teach us a skill we want to know. But when it comes to life, we may balk at completely following the directions of the Master and Creator of life himself. It's too hard, we may say, or we'll buckle down later, we're doing all right, nobody's perfect, or nobody has really told us how. We may say that those blessings and rules are for the bishop, or God doesn't know we live when there are so many billions of people.

Our hearts haven't been touched by Christ's spirit when we think these things. It can be said we are not converted to him and his teachings. We have not been living righteously enough to have the Holy Ghost witness to us of the validity of the principles of the gospel. Then we aren't motivated or instructed enough to live by them.

In the face of all this, there seem to be certain steps to take to arrive at a point of change or conversion or righteousness unto happiness. These steps are "The Six Steps of Change":

First, we must come to know God and respect God as our supreme authority, as the one who sets the standard we are to follow.

Second, we need to know who we are, why God cares about us, and what role we are here to play. We must look upon our inner core, the spiritual self or essence of intelligence that always has been. As we discern our relationship to Christ, we'll come to

21

know our own mission. Then we'll see reason for trying to become more like him. As we compare ourselves to him, we will surely see a vast difference between what he is and what we are. We will see there is a need to change.

Third, exactly what does it mean if we succeed in changing to one spiritually born again? Is there special reward? And if we don't succeed in becoming born again, or Christlike, will there be punishment involved? What need to change is there that is strong enough to motivate a mighty effort on our part?

Fourth, we need information to act upon. We must move from vague generalities to specific goals. Understanding old principles and new information can be highly motivating when we have a definite goal we are working on. But what do we do? Where will we find such information?

Fifth, we must establish a system of values to operate under. It has been said that where your treasure is, there your heart is also. So what the heart is concerned with, the mind follows. Knowledge determines values, and values influence behavior. It seems obvious that setting the heart upon eternal values protects one against wallowing in earthbound pleasures. If we put our value upon the things of Christ, we are more likely to become like him.

Sixth, change requires commitment. We must be determined to take the course of action necessary to bring about the change in ourselves. We have to try, apply, and act upon certain information to prove its worth. We must plant the seed and help it flourish.

As we try, we do move ever closer to becoming the manner of being Christ is. So now, let's go on to a discussion of each of these six basic principles, to put them to work for us as we try to change.

STEP ONE:
COMING TO TRULY KNOW HIM

*A*nd this is life eternal, that they might know thee the only true God, and Jesus Christ, whom thou hast sent." (John 17:3.)

Does our knowledge of God impel us to keep his command-ments and to strive constantly to know more of his word that we are to live by? (See John 2:3-4.) Let us talk of him whom we would come to know, to whom we would become truly converted.

Jesus said, "Come unto me." (Matthew 11:28.)

He said, "Learn of me." (Matthew 11:29.)

And he said, "Follow thou me." (2 Nephi 31:10.)

Unless we learn of Christ, we cannot follow him. If we do not follow him, we cannot be spiritually born again. If we are not spiritually born again through conversion to him, we cannot have the joy of his companionship.

During the Savior's ministry on the American continent, he was deeply troubled because of the wickedness of the people of the house of Israel. He knelt in the presence of the multitude whom he had been teaching. Then, out loud, he prayed for them.

They heard him speak to the Father many marvelous things in their behalf. When he had finished, he arose from the earth where he had knelt. But the people who had knelt with him were so overcome with joy at what they had seen and heard in their own behalf that they didn't move. Finally, Jesus tenderly bade them to arise. And then they too arose, and everyone listened and wept as he said to them, "Blessed are ye because of your faith. And now behold, my joy is full." (3 Nephi 17:20.)

Then Jesus wept. And in an act of the sweetest kind, which warmed the hearts of all the parents, family members, friends, and loved ones gathered there, he took their little children, one by one, and blessed them and prayed unto the Father for them. When he had done this, he wept again and presented them before the people, and said to them, "Behold your little ones." (3 Nephi 17:23.)

Wouldn't we like to have our own personal experience with the Lord? Surely there is something to be learned about this from the example of the little ones whom the Lord loves so much. They are innocent, responsive, believing. For example, there was a little family of three small boys whose mother had recently passed away. The valiant father had tried repeatedly to explain this poignant loss to his sons. He used all the means of the gospel and of good teaching and of prayer, and set an example of faith himself. During a family home evening, he described the wonders of the world that a loving Heavenly Father had prepared, trying to show the boys how much God had done and how very good he was. Then he described God as loving us so much that he wanted to make a place for us to live that was exquisite in every way; and he told them that their mother was living now with Heavenly Father in a place even more lovely. The father went on to talk of the beginnings of spring; of birds preparing nests, getting ready for new family members; of violets coming up; of snow-capped mountains. Snow-capped mountains? To California children this was the most marvelous of all. The father knew when he had a captive audience. A teaching moment was at hand. He carried it a step further and determined they'd go out in the world on a field trip and see close up the beauties God had given them.

Everyone was at the car waiting for the three-year-old, who had been scrounging in the back closets for high boots suitable for a real adventure. He finally clomped out the door, took a deep breath, and threw his little arms toward the sky. "Hello, Heavenly Father! Hello!" Then he smiled his broadest smile at the prospects of the excitement ahead. For him God was very real, and very much worth loving after all.

Such moments in life remind us of our own love for the Savior and for God the Father.

As we become devoted disciples of Christ, we will come to respect him, to love him, and to know that what he has told us to do to return to his presence is right. We will not be able to do other than change ourselves to become like him.

When we are trying to learn anything, we are better off studying under the finest teacher we can find. In the matter of learning how to be exalted, the example we look to, the model we pattern our lives after, must qualify in the ultimate measure of perfection. Only one such being answers that demand. That being is, of course, the Lord and Savior Jesus Christ.

As we take steps to experience the mighty change in our lives, we will find proper inspiration and guidance from Christ, who cares so much about our success. Christ knows us. He created us and established the plan of life and the method of redemption. He is our teacher and friend. He loves us and wants us to know the joy of his presence. He will not lead us astray, nor can he.

We can feel the beginning of that respect for God which must come before love by beginning to respect admirable people with whom we come in contact. From our youth, we can look at the people we have loved. The more Christlike people are, the more appealing they are. It is wholesome to think about those who have had a powerful influence for good upon us. Parents are usually our first models. A friend, teacher, athletic hero, church figure, or noble neighbor can be an example we have followed.

A young boy respects a ballplayer because of his ability, and wants to be just like him in every other way too. And if he is following a fine ballplayer or has wise parents who guide him along the way from hero to hero, the boy grows up and emulates other fine models, such as his bishop or his mission president. Then eventually comes the mighty step toward emulating Christ, a step that must come before a life is ready for truly effective service on earth and dwelling in that ideal setting of heaven.

We must remember how important it is to transfer our devotion from heroes, people, even prophets, to the Savior himself. For it has been said to us, "Cursed is he that putteth his trust in man, or maketh flesh his arm, or shall hearken unto the precepts of men, save their precepts shall be given by the power of the Holy Ghost." (2 Nephi 28:31.)

A classic example comes to us in Alma's experience with Korihor, the antichrist who was leading people astray in ancient America (about B.C. 74). When Korihor was brought before Alma and the chief judge, he reviled violently against priests, teachers, and others who labor in remembrance of Christ. The scripture describes the exchange that went on between Alma and this wicked, blinded man:

"And then Alma said unto him [Korihor]: Believest thou that there is a God?

"And he answered, Nay.

"Now Alma said unto him: Will ye deny again that there is a God, and also deny the Christ? For behold, I say unto you, I know there is a God, and also that Christ shall come.

"And now what evidence have ye that there is no God, or that Christ cometh not? I say unto you that ye have none, save it be your word only.

"But, behold, I have all things as a testimony that these things are true; and ye also have all things as a testimony unto you that they are true; and will ye deny them? Believest thou that these things are true?"

But Korihor was possessed of a lying spirit and had put off the Spirit of God to such an extent that the devil had full power over him. This Alma knew, and he commented upon it. Korihor said he wanted a tangible sign that there was a God. But Alma replied: "Thou hast had signs enough; will ye tempt your God? Will ye say, Show unto me a sign, when ye have the testimony of all these thy brethren, and also all the holy prophets? The scriptures are laid before thee, yea, and all things denote there is a God; yea, even the earth, and all things that are upon the face of it, yea, and its motion, yea, and also all the planets which move in their regular form do witness that there is a Supreme Creator.

"And yet do ye go about, leading away the hearts of this people, testifying unto them there is no God?"

But Korihor would not receive the spirit of direction, the Spirit of the Lord, because he had given in to wickedness. He persisted in wanting a sign before he would respect the notion of a God. We all know the pathetic turn of events. God did, in fact, give him a sign. He was struck dumb. Later, because he still couldn't speak, Korihor wrote, "I know that nothing save it were the power of God could bring this upon me; yea, and I also knew that there was a God. But behold, the devil hath deceived me. . . ."

God did not remove the curse from Korihor, because he might have continued to lead people astray. Korihor lost his crown and died a pitiful beggar. (Alma 30:37-60.)

The story may read like a movie script, but there is real value in it for us as we come to grips with our own testimony of Christ. Alma points out to Korihor three valuable ways any of us can know of God's existence and goodness:

1. We have the testimony of the prophets and others.

2. We have the scriptures in which all things are declared and which witness of Christ.

3. We have proof of a divine Creator in the marvels of nature.

If we would, we can learn from those who have seen Christ, those who have worked for him, and those who serve him now. We can study the scriptures, prayerfully ponder their meaning, and grow in understanding of his whole plan of life for us. We can drink in the beauties of nature and have the sweetness of life well up within us as did the motherless boy going on the field trip.

Then we can turn to God himself and ask him for the gift of testimony that he lives. We can put to the test the promise given in James 1:5: "If any of you lack wisdom, let him ask of God, that giveth to all men liberally, and upbraideth not; and it shall be given him."

Joseph Smith took the Lord at his word. He prayed, and he received the answer in the form of a powerful vision of the Father and the Son. We may not have the purity of being nor be called to such an important mission as the Prophet Joseph, but we can get our own kind of answer. Countless persons can testify that prayers of this kind have been answered with the undeniable witness that Christ lives, that he is God the Creator, and that we are not only safe but smart in following after him closely.

Elohim, or God the Eternal Father, is an exalted, glorified personage. He is an entity in the way we understand a person to be. He is an individual with a tangible, resurrected body of flesh and bones. (D&C 130:22.) He is fulfilled and perfected. He is the literal Father of the spirits of all men. We have it within us to ultimately become like him.

God is the Father of Jehovah, or Jesus, his Firstborn in the spirit world and his only child begotten in the flesh. Jesus, as the Son of God, was supreme among the spirit children in the pre-earth existence. He followed the direction of the Father in creating this world. He was foreordained before this world was to be our Savior, our mediator (between man and God), and our ultimate teacher and example. He came to earth and filled his mission of teaching, blessing, and atoning for mankind. He was crucified and rose again on the third day. He lives now as an exalted, glorified, resurrected being. And we are to try to become more like him.

One day, like the little boy going out in the beautiful world, we might say to ourselves, "Hello, Heavenly Father!" He has promised us the privilege of seeing him face to face if we learn of him and follow him. (D&C 93:1.)

STEP TWO:
COMING TO KNOW OURSELVES

Our feeling of self-worth grows and swells significantly when at last we come to believe that we are, in fact, children of God. There is a spark of the divine in us. We have spiritual roots. "The Spirit itself beareth witness with our spirit, that we are the children of God." (Romans 8:16.)

Knowing who God is and what he has done for us gives us a precious perspective about our own worth. This is the next step in accomplishing the mighty change in our hearts. God loves us not because we are great, but because *he* is great. He has said we can become like him. He has dedicated his life to helping us. We are his children, and he wants us to return to him.

Why not change to become like him and reap the blessings here and hereafter that he has promised us in return? Perhaps we can better envision God's love for us by the following example.

It was the young father's first child. His wife's parents were serving a mission abroad, and so his own mother had accompanied them to the hospital for this momentous occasion. The father went into the delivery room to watch the miracle of birth.

The grandmother waited just outside the door. At the first sound of the baby's cry, the door flew open and the excited young man rushed out to announce the news.

"It's a boy! A boy! And I just love him!"

He had hardly had time to check his new baby over, much less build up any kind of relationship with him, but he loved him already. The baby was something he had helped to create. Therefore, he was worth loving.

The grandmother looked at her son and smiled knowingly. "Isn't it wonderful? Do you know that is exactly the way I feel about you?"

"It is?" The son was surprised. His mother loved him the way he loved that new boychild in there? How could that be? He looked at her, somewhat embarrassed. He didn't feel the same way about her as he did about that remarkable little bundle.

"Yes," she said. "You are my firstborn. I love you freely, as you love your own baby. But just remember, he probably won't feel much different toward you than you do toward me. My reward is that you love your children as I love you. Though it may be hard to believe at this moment, your heart will expand in parenthood, and you'll love all your children as much as this one. There's another perspective to this situation too. Our capacity to love our children cannot begin to compare with Heavenly Father's. You now have a little idea of how much Heavenly Father loves you. One day you'll learn to love Heavenly Father as your boy will learn to love you."

Important lessons in love were learned that morning in a hospital corridor. A parent goes on loving a child whether love is returned or not. The heart expands with boundless love, and each additional child is welcomed the same as the first. Unselfish love is Christlike love. It knows no bounds. It seems incredible until the experiences of life and love thrust it upon us. Then it is like a great door of understanding opening for us. In such a setting, we can begin to appreciate the scripture found in Doctrine and Covenants 18:10, "Remember the worth of souls is great in the sight of God."

Someone has defined love as ultimate concern. Surely, our

Heavenly Father cares in the extreme what happens to us, just as we care about our own offspring. The Savior's primary concern on earth, the full sweep of his mission, proved the worth of souls before God. He came that men might have life, and have it more abundantly. He taught the value of the individual over tradition, customs, rules, and laws, in a day when the Pharisees were concerned over the letter of the law.

Christ taught there is no rest from the work of saving souls. He taught that the publican, the sinner, and the saint alike are counted precious before God and that the gospel is for the sacred purpose of molding the soul to make it ready for celestial life and all the joyous blessings God has in store for us.

Christ taught the great concern of God for all men, including the lost and the low. He used three powerful parables to give us insight into how precious everyone is to him. In the parable of the lost sheep, the shepherd left the others to find the sheep that had strayed. He brought it back to the fold and cried, "Rejoice with me; for I have found my sheep which was lost." (Luke 15:6.) In the parable of the lost coin, a search located that money which was lost, and again we read, "Rejoice with me; for I have found the piece which I had lost." (Luke 15:9.) In the parable of the lost son, the prodigal's wayward ways lost for him all that was valuable in life. He finally turned homeward, repentant, and his father, seeing him far off, "ran, and fell on his neck, and kissed him." (Luke 15:20.)

In each case, the Savior compared that which was lost to the soul of man and pointedly declared that there would likewise be much joy among the angels over one sinner who repents.

We cannot study the parables or the life of the Savior and his ministry without being warmed to our personal value to our Heavenly Father, his Son Jesus Christ, and the heavenly hosts. In fact, the scriptures remind us that God so loved us that he sent his *only* begotten Son to atone for our sins, to suffer, to be crucified, and to die for us. Salvation now is ours. (John 3:16.)

When we finally become aware of our noble being, of the fact that the Lord loves us enough to die for us and that he is waiting to be gracious in all things to us; when we begin to understand the plan of life and the principles God has given us to live it, something begins to happen within us. The mighty change is underway. Little by little, line upon line, our understanding and capacities increase. We take another step toward exaltation.

Let us consider some factors in the plan:

1. We respect and revere God and his Son Jesus Christ.

2. We were created in their image and are heirs to all the glorious things they enjoy.

3. We have the potential to become like them.

4. They love us and want us to succeed in this effort.

5. They devised a system to help us.

6. They have given us the gift of the Holy Ghost.

What worth we are! How humble, thankful, and motivated we should be in the face of these facts! We who are just a little lower than the angels (Psalm 8:5) can become like God. We are of infinite worth.

With all the similarity among mankind, each of us is still unique. Each of us is counted above all things. The Lord has said he is as mindful of each of us as he is of each blade of grass and the sparrow's fall.

Each of us has a lineage that is impressive. Spiritually, we stem from God. Physically, we are descendants of father Abraham and are entitled to all the blessings of God promised Abraham's entire posterity in their worthiness. Our own close family ties enrich our lives beyond expression. And we are indebted to all who have gone before us and laid foundations for us to build upon.

Unique gifts of the Spirit are ours to help us on our journey through life and in our efforts at becoming perfect. Besides our innate talents, we are heir to blessings, ordinances, principles, programs, and a whole army of people to lead, guide, and be examples to us.

There is still another marvelous advantage we have. We are entitled to a personal patriarchal blessing to give us comfort, strength, guidance, and information about our life's mission. This blessing from God is reserved for only a fraction of the people of the world. Only one in good standing as a member of the church of Jesus Christ is entitled to have hands placed upon his head by an ordained patriarch and, through the power of the priesthood of God, receive this special blessing.

Each blessing is unique. Lineage is declared and promises are foretold. In a letter to stake presidents, dated June 28, 1957, President David O. McKay wrote the following:

"Patriarchal blessings contemplate an inspired declaration of the lineage of the recipient, and also, where so moved upon by the Spirit, an inspired and prophetic statement of the life mission of the recipient, together with such blessings, cautions, and admonitions as the patriarch may be prompted to give for the accomplishment of such life's mission, it being always made clear that the realization of all promised blessings is conditioned upon faithfulness to the gospel of our Lord, whose servant the patriarch is. All such blessings are recorded and generally only one such blessing should be adequate for each person's life. The sacred nature of the patriarchal blessing must of necessity urge all patriarchs to most earnest solicitation of divine guidance for their prophetic utterances and superior wisdom for cautions and admonition."

Studying our patriarchal blessing constantly, especially in times of trial, decision, depression, or temptation, will quickly give us the vision of who we really are, what our relationship with God is, and what his will for us is. It can be most motivating in our efforts to become more like the Savior. It can comfort us when we feel inadequate, unloved, or unworthy. It can be a guide to help us make choices.

There is still another facet to our lives that is a bolster in experiencing the mighty change of heart. It is that, as members of The Church of Jesus Christ of Latter-day Saints, we are part of a chosen people. As such, we have certain rights and responsibilities. God is, of course, no respecter of persons. It is because he loves all his children that he has a "chosen" people. These are persons chosen to carry his standard before men, to testify of him in a special manner, to be a light to his children in darkness. We in the Church today have taken upon us his name and his work. We have marvelous blessings from him to aid us in our efforts.

"I the Lord have called thee in righteousness, and will hold thine hand, and will keep thee, and give thee for a covenant of the people, for a light of the Gentiles; To open the blind eyes, to bring out the prisoners from the prison, and them that sit in darkness out of the prison house." (Isaiah 42:6-7.) This scripture is for us in our day.

How thankful we should be to be counted among a people who are called in this dispensation to spread the word among the living and to do the work for the salvation of the dead! We are a small band compared to all the rest of the world, but we have a work to do for others as well as ourselves.

So, we are children of God. Each of us is endowed with certain unique personal gifts, is a recipient of special gospel blessings, and is a member of a covenant people with a vitally important job to do.

With all of this going for us, we should marvel at our station in life. Lethargy and despondency should have no place in us. Instead, we should be motivated to reap the fullness of our privileged condition by continuing to repent, change, and beautify our lives.

Consider this quotation from C. S. Lewis in his book *Mere Christianity:*

"Imagine yourself as a living house. God comes in to rebuild that house. At first, perhaps, you can understand what He is doing. He is getting the drains right and stopping the leaks in the roof and so on: you knew that those jobs needed doing and so you are not surprised. But presently he starts knocking the house about in a way that hurts abominably and does not seem to make sense. What on earth is He up to? The explanation is that He is building quite a different house from the one you thought of— throwing out a new wing here, putting on an extra floor there, running up towers, making courtyards. You thought you were going to be made into a decent little cottage: but He is building a palace." (New York: Macmillan, 1952, p. 174.)

What a blessing to be so loved by a Heavenly Father! If he as well as our earthly parents cares so much about what happens to us, surely we should care enough about ourselves to continue to grow and change.

The excitement of the whole adventure of experiencing the mighty change is what happens to us and to our lives in the process. We come to know God and to understand his purposes and love for us. Then we come to know ourselves, our gifts, our worth, and our position as children of God. That's the second step in the process of personal change.

STEP THREE:
FEELING THE NEED TO CHANGE

Let's look over our shoulder. Who is stalking our path armed with commands to straighten up, relax, stay home, get out more, save money, spend money, train vigorously, eat out, diet, start smiling, enlist, resign, stop complaining, start changing?

Who is dogging our steps with this or that advice for help?

A whole society of advertisers, psychologists, self-help experts, and well-meaning friends who have problems enough of their own, that's who!

It might just be, however, that one of those voices behind us giving us counsel that requires our changing is the prophet, our bishop, or a loving parent who dares to tell us the truth about ourself. Are we irritated? Or are we listening? Maybe they have a point.

Let's go back to the creation of mankind, to the Garden of Eden, and make an analogy. Even Adam had someone checking up on him. The Lord, bringing Adam out of hiding, called, "Where art thou?" (Genesis 3:9.) And the question comes echoing across the eons to rest squarely in our own hearts.

Where are we? Where are we in terms of personal growth, personal peace, self-esteem, worthiness? Where are we in our pursuit of happiness and in chalking up qualities compatible with a heavenlike life? Where are we in self-control? What kind of habits have we given in to? Where are we with respect to family spirit and professional success?

Where are we in our relationship with the Lord? Are we keeping all of his commandments so we might always have his Spirit to be with us?

In 1 John 1:8, we read, "If we say that we have no sin, we deceive ourselves, and the truth is not in us." And in 1 Kings 8:46, we are reminded that "there is no man that sinneth not." There is not one of us who can't improve. It might seem an insurmountable task to become like Christ, but we learn that through Christ who strengthens us we can do all things. (Philippians 4:13.)

It really doesn't take a lot of harrowing up of the soul to know that most of us don't yet have a toe in the celestial kingdom. We aren't even overwhelming our neighbors with radiant countenances reflecting Christ's image, which probably means we haven't experienced the "mighty change" in our hearts.

On good days, we may feel God's approval for a wise or kind thing we have done. Sometimes a friend stands in testimony meeting, gentle with the Spirit, and we are warmed with the remembrance of sacred things. Sometimes our need of the moment is so great that our knees bend, our heads bow before God, and, with a contrite heart, we pour out our feelings. Then we feel the walls and ceilings disappear as we pray.

When we discover where we are, we need to consider where we could be. Where we have been can be wiped out through repentance, if necessary. It is where we are going and what we can become that deserves our attention.

We can quit smoking. We can find new friends. We can pay an honest tithe. We can overlook our companion's annoying mannerisms. We can go before the bishop for a full confession to wipe the slate clean. We can!

You will recall the dramatic moments following King Benjamin's sermon when he "cast his eyes round about on the multitude, and behold they had fallen to the earth, for the fear of the Lord had come upon them.

"And they had viewed themselves in their own carnal state, even less than the dust of the earth. And they all cried aloud with one voice, saying: O have mercy, and apply the atoning blood of Christ that we may receive forgiveness of our sins, and our hearts may be purified; for we believe in Jesus Christ, the Son of God, who created heaven and earth, and all things; who shall come down among the children of men.

"And it came to pass that after they had spoken these words the Spirit of the Lord came upon them, and they were filled with joy, having received a remission of their sins, and having peace of conscience, because of the exceeding faith which they had in Jesus Christ who should come, according to the words which king Benjamin had spoken unto them." (Mosiah 4:1-3.)

Therein lies the clue to true change, conversion to Christ. How beautiful the day when a person's conversion brings him to his knees before God in repentant awareness and a determination to qualify according to God's commandments!

When we ourselves taste of the joy of righteous living or witness it in others, we become motivated to change. An example of this is a mission experience. The same thing is true of sorrow. If we have been wracked with the hell of sin, have awakened in the night with our heart pounding, perspiration beading our body, our fears choking us, or if we have watched another go through the anxiety of guilt, we are motivated to change. We all need to change in some way, but we know that true change doesn't occur until we want to change, until the spirit directs the body. The need to change has to be of more importance than the ease of staying the same.

Needing to change and wanting to change do not necessarily crowd one's awareness at the same moment nor with the same effectiveness. Synonyms of the word *want* are wish, inclination, whim, longing, intent. Need is a stronger word and implies a more motivating force—necessity, obligation, compulsion, predetermination, urgency, requirement.

But self-sufficiency or prosperity can lull us into contentment and take away any seeming need to change. Isn't it interesting that we don't miss something until we're deprived of it? We don't think of a coat until the temperature drops. Fast Sunday is the day we're most hungry. Walking is duly appreciated only when we've injured a leg. Counting our blessings before we're deprived of them is a good way, however, to become aware of our situation in life. To the person halfway down the road to perfection, his need may be that of awareness of how much he has and how much he ought to be doing with what the Lord has blessed him.

The higher level of change is to become so converted to Christ that we not only strive to keep his commandments, but we also try to be like him in every way possible. And then we want to help others lift themselves to greater personal perfection. We change for the better as we have an experience with change by helping others. Who changes the most, the missionary or the people with whom he works? Who gets the most from the class, the student or the teacher? What wonderful worlds would open for single persons, for example, if they were to get outside themselves in service to others.

Each of us falls into a kind of category. We might be rebellious and hard-hearted and not realize the value of Christ in our life. Or we might go along our complacent way, attending meetings and making donations, but solving our problems by the standards of the world and not according to Christ. We might get divorced instead of working out our marital problems with Christ's help. We might succumb to sin instead of withstanding the adversary. At best, we might quarrel in the family and gossip about the neighbors instead of living in a beautiful "what if" kind of society.

We claim to be followers of Christ. But what do we more than others? (See Matthew 5:47.)

We didn't come to earth just to exist. We were placed here to become perfect like unto God. Therefore, the feeling that perhaps we want to change or even need to change really is too mild. We *must* change! Only Christ was without flaw. As children of God, surely his plan in putting us here on earth was for a mighty purpose. The trials, the testings, the learnings, the gropings, the changes we must go through are all for the purpose that we might grow sufficiently to be ready to receive life eternal, life more abundant.

We must serve and give and forgive with all of our heart, might, mind, and strength. We must know how to control our circumstances and endure our trials with equanimity. We must try to abstain from evil acting and thinking. We must, in fact, *be* pure. We must be on fire about the gospel, about Christ, about lengthening our stride in obedience to the prophet's counsel.

It takes true humility to face the truth of our need to change toward Christlikeness. We must be willing to listen to the voices that speak for our good, that speak of those truths which lead us toward exaltation. We must remain teachable before prophets, priesthood leaders, and goodly parents. We must mark the measure of our ability to implement gospel principles in daily life, lest we fall too far short in the final act. To be humble and seek God for help, to listen to his chosen servants, and to be moved upon to change our lives accordingly are of prime importance.

There have been those who have listened to the wrong voices. There have been people who have respected the wrong leader and have lost their birthright. The scriptures are full of such rebels. History is replete with such examples of poor judgment.

But we have our agency to choose to whom we shall listen, whom we shall follow. We have the Holy Ghost, which can be cultivated and called upon to guide us in such critical deliberation.

To clarify how we need to change, we can follow these suggestions:

1. We can continually compare ourselves to Christ and his word as given to us in the scriptures. What has God said we must be like? He has said we should come unto him and "be perfected" in him and "deny [ourselves] of all ungodliness." (Moroni 10:32.) How are we to respond to daily situations and trials of life? What responses are expected of us? What commandments are we to

keep? What guidance has been given to us based on eternal laws that will, if kept, bring us the desired blessings for all eternity?

2. We can seek the will of God. Humbly, and in faith, we can go before our Heavenly Father in need. "Draw near unto me and I will draw near unto you." (D&C 88:63.) He wants us to make it back into his presence. He is our creator, and we are of great worth to him. He knows us. We can find his will for us by listening to his prophets, studying our patriarchal blessing and the scriptures, and living so that we may have the companionship and gifts of the Holy Ghost.

3. We can look inward upon our own heart. Examining our center core, facing squarely to our life and our attitudes can reveal our strengths and weaknesses. How do we feel about the wife who won't lose weight, the husband who won't get active in the church, the neighbor who lets his dog roam at night? What are our feelings about God when we say that he hasn't heard our prayers, hasn't sent someone for us to marry, hasn't helped us succeed in business, or hasn't healed our arthritis?

4. We can start changing. We can get some goals by deciding to change that thing in us which is most jeopardizing our spiritual well-being. We will need information to act upon, and that brings us to the next principle of experiencing the mighty change.

STEP FOUR:
INFORMATION TO ACT UPON

builder uses a set of plans to follow in constructing a house. A seamstress uses a pattern to guide her in making a dress. A child studying the piano and a swimmer preparing for the Olympic tryouts need instructions to help them reach their goals. Families improve when household chores are clearly defined. Flourishing businesses have job descriptions for their employees.

So it is with life. The Lord, Creator of this life, has given us information to act upon that is guaranteed by him to guide us safely to our goal of life eternal. This information is the word of God. It is not only truth revealed and power bestowed upon earthly leaders, but also a program of appropriate action and conduct for every individual member. It is a blessing for the person who wants to become like Christ.

Wouldn't it be ridiculous to be a spectator or participant in an athletic event in which the players dressed up in basketball suits, carried tennis rackets, and marched out on a football field to play baseball by soccer rules? Yet there are some of us who go through life as foolishly. We turn to the tenets of men instead of God when it is his game—a very serious game with eternal overtones.

When the Holy Ghost filled the people following the miracle of Pentecost, Peter explained to them what had happened; and, "when they heard this, they were pricked in their heart, and said . . . what shall we do?" (Acts 2:37.)

Christ delivered his magnificent Sermon on the Mount to the multitude and then summed up with these words instructions for a grander life than they'd ever known before: "What do ye more than others?" (Matthew 5:47.)

Many good people of the earth know only the law of Moses to live by, and only a portion who "know" it live it. There is yet a smaller portion of the world who try to live the gospel the Savior taught when he told the people they were to do more than love their neighbors—they were to love their enemies. In our time, Christ has revealed to his servants on earth that he wants his children to live even more strictly and beautifully. We are required to love all mankind!

And there are other instructions, other information that we must act upon in these latter days. Do we know what things we must do as disciples of Christ? Do we, personally, have the necessary knowledge for exaltation? Do we know what the covenants of the temple are all about? Do we have information to act upon that will prepare us for an interview for a temple recommend, a patriarchal blessing, a mission call?

Do we understand what it is that we must do so we will, in fact, love all mankind as we are commanded to do?

Do we know how to become converted unto the Lord?

The answers, the instructions, the information to act upon can be found in the holy scriptures and through the Lord's appointed servants on the earth. In addition, he has given us the Holy Ghost to help us retain, recall, reevaluate, reaffirm, and reuse the information. He has given us this gift. It is up to us to receive and use it.

Nephi taught that the scriptures were designed—

1. To help us gain a testimony of Christ. We must know, not

just assume, that he is the authority to whom we are to listen, the one after whom we are to model our lives, and that his word is for our benefit.

2. For our profit and learning, so we might get truth to act upon that will qualify us for life's greatest blessings here and hereafter.

3. To persuade us to do good and motivate us to experiment upon the word of the Lord so we might learn its infinite value in our efforts toward constant personal progress.

If we carefully read Nephi's instructions to his people, we will find enlightenment for our own situation. He said: "I suppose that ye ponder somewhat in your hearts concerning that which ye should do after ye have entered in by the way. But, behold, why do ye ponder these things in your hearts? . . . wherefore, I [say] unto you, feast upon the words of Christ; for behold, the words of Christ will tell you all things what ye should do. . . . [If] ye cannot understand them it will be because ye ask not, neither do ye knock, wherefore, ye are not brought into the light, but must perish in the dark. . . . [If] ye will . . . receive the Holy Ghost, it will show unto you all things what ye should do. Behold, this is the doctrine of Christ. . . ." (2 Nephi 32:1-6.)

The Savior himself told us, "Learn of me, and listen to my words; walk in the meekness of my Spirit, and you shall have peace in me." (D&C 19:23.) He then gave some specific information on personal behavior before pronouncing the sweet promise, "Pray always, and I will pour out my Spirit upon you, and great shall be your blessing—yea, even more than if you should obtain treasures of earth and corruptibleness to the extent thereof. Behold, canst thou read this without rejoicing and lifting up thy heart for gladness?" (D&C 19:38-39.)

It's all there in the scriptures. The Lord has said so. We can determine from them whom to marry, how to be patient with others, how to be sustained in trials, how to get help in our projects, and how to discern the needs of a loved one. We can know exactly how to go through the healing process of repentance. We can understand the importance of temple work, food storage, missionary effort, and resisting the entertainments of the world. We can increase in compassion and charity and Christlike performance when we're deeply hurt. We can forgive and forget.

As we study the scriptures, we have been told by the Lord to "ask God, the Eternal Father, in the name of Christ, if these things are not true; and if [we] shall ask with a sincere heart, with real intent, having faith in Christ, he will manifest the truth of it unto [us], by the power of the Holy Ghost. And by the power of the Holy Ghost [we] may know the truth of all things." (Moroni 10:4-5.) We can know, deep within us, that the Lord's doctrine for us to live by is true. It is the way we'll be happiest. We can ask God and obtain our own unshakable testimony. We can ask for what we need, obtain direction for our lives, and receive blessings as we prove ourselves worthy, step by step. There is no more marvelous system for our joy than the gospel of Jesus Christ in its fullness.

To obtain this information, we must study the scriptures, listen to the prophets, read the manuals and periodicals, participate in growing experiences provided by the Church, counsel with other members in good standing, teach one another, and pray mightily unto God for enlightenment and the ability to retain what we're learning.

We cannot afford to miss out on the word of the Lord. If we find ourselves at odds with a principle or counsel from the prophet, it is because we don't understand. The prophet will not be wrong. He is inspired by God.

There have been people through the ages of time who just haven't received this message. Cain is an example. The Nephites following the golden era described in 4 Nephi are examples. There were the children in King Benjamin's day who didn't understand his sermon and who grew up hard-hearted and unrighteous. Laman and Lemuel, Lehi's sons, murmured and finally led their families into rebellion.

There have been church leaders and family members—even some close to prophets—who haven't seemed to have understanding sufficient to become committed to the gospel pattern so they might grow to full conversion. Instead, they have fallen away as dissenters.

We today are not as valiant as we should or could be. There are people getting divorced who should know better. There are some succumbing to the evils of sexual sins yet professing to be "active in the Church." And so on, in sad story after sad story.

We have been told time and again (but sometimes we forget) that there is a law irrevocably decreed, before this earth was, upon which every blessing is predicated. (D&C 130:20-21.) If we want a certain blessing, we must abide by its law.

Knowing the law becomes exceedingly important, doesn't it? We cannot underestimate this fact. The Prophet Joseph said we can't be saved in ignorance. To be saved, we must know the gospel. We may have gone to church, opened the scriptures along the way, and in other ways been exposed to the gospel as ward members, teachers, or missionaries—but sometimes, the meaning or facts have escaped us. We may have been out of the mood or felt no personal need at the moment for what we were reading or hearing. We may have been taught by an uninspired teacher, or led by a poor example, or not given good perspective in true principles at home. We may have been so caught up in the things of the world that we forgot what the law for a blessing was, forgot what the Lord said we should do. Instead of saying, "Which of my Heavenly Father's principles will help me now in this time of crisis," we make a foolish mistake.

The Savior knew we'd have our struggles in learning. This is why he has continued to strive with us. He wants us to make it. Let's consider the parable of the sower. It gives us powerful insight to remind us to get the word and nourish it.

"When any one heareth the word of the kingdom, and understandeth it not, then cometh the wicked one, and catcheth away that which was sown in his heart. This is he which received seed [or the word] by the way side.

"But he that received the seed into stony places, the same is he that heareth the word, and anon with joy receiveth it;

"Yet hath he not root in himself, but dureth for a while: for when tribulation or persecution ariseth because of the word, by and by he is offended.

"He also that received seed among the thorns is he that

heareth the word; and the care of this world, and the deceitfulness of riches, choke the word, and he becometh unfruitful.

"But he that received seed into the good ground is he that heareth the word, and understandeth it; which also beareth fruit, and bringeth forth, some an hundredfold, some sixty, some thirty." (Matthew 13:19-23.)

How do we receive the word?

Alma's mission to his brethren the Zoramites was largely unsuccessful. The word of God had fallen upon hard hearts. He was grieved. They had all had essentially the same instruction in gospel principles, yet some had become like Alma and Amulek, while others had become dissenters, builders of Rameumpton. As Alma returned home, he wondered about his own family. Had they merely heard the word, or had they understood it unto their salvation? And so he called his sons together that "he might give unto them every one his charge, separately, concerning the things pertaining unto righteousness." (Alma 35:16.)

Christ was in a weakened state after fasting forty days in the wilderness to prepare for his mission. It was then that the adversary moved in. But the temptations were not heeded. Christ was victorious as a man. Later, on the cross, when he voluntarily gave up his life, he proved victorious.

We are to follow in his steps and become perfect. When we are in a weakened state, discouraged, depressed, justifying our actions because of deprivation, or feeling frustration and self-pity, that is when the adversary will move in upon us with temptation. We must stand. We must have information to act upon that will change our values so our behavior will be appropriate as children of God.

Strength and success come to us in our efforts at perfection when we move from distant, general goals to specific, immediate action. For example, a vague self-promise to improve in living the gospel is not nearly so commanding for performance as is a covenant made before the Lord in his holy house to keep the law of chastity. A casual declaration following general conference that "I'm going to be a good church member" might bring fruition. But a specific attack on a personal problem—"I'm going to pay a full tithing today"—will bring more effective results. Moving from general attitudes to specific action is more sound.

The gospel gives us information that is specific. We can come to it line upon line and act upon it as we understand it to help us meet the tests of life. Then we, like Christ, will grow from grace to grace. You see, first we learn to keep the Ten Commandments. Then we apply to our lives the higher Christian principles as they were taught by the Savior during his ministry on earth. And finally, for exaltation, we must live by the fullness of his word as revealed in these latter days and participate in the saving priesthood ordinances.

Our challenge, then, is to take every opportunity to learn the word of the Lord and let it fall upon hearts and minds ready to receive it, nourish it, treasure it, use it, and benefit from it.

STEP FIVE:
ESTABLISHING NEW VALUES

The process by which a change of heart occurs begins when we diligently seek to know Heavenly Father and his Son Jesus Christ. When we have a personal crisis or a spiritual experience, our knowledge of God increases, and often we are moved to take another look at ourselves. Comparing ourselves to the Savior, we know we must do some changing to be more like him. If we want certain blessings he has for us, we know we must do certain things. We begin to recognize our worth to God enough to heed his instructions for us. Then by studying, searching, praying, reaching out, and, finally, experimenting upon his word, the miracle begins.

When at last we are truly touched by the gospel of Jesus Christ and begin to experiment upon his word in our daily lives, our values are different. This is an important level in accomplishing the mighty change. Now our long-range goal of eternal joy becomes a specific and immediate goal. We want the presence of God in our lives now as well as after we die. The fruits of righteous living begin to taste sweet to us. Life still isn't a rose garden, but we are learning to cope and to accept.

51

At last we are growing in the gospel. We are beginning to value peace in this life and to hope we might have the Spirit of Christ with us always. We value spiritual things more than we value monetary or temporal delights. We'd rather be honest than steal. We'd rather pay an honest tithe than use the money for new car payments. We'd rather get our food storage than live in a higher rent district. We'd rather go on a mission than accept a scholarship.

We have come to love the Lord so much that we are beginning to love his children. We are careful not to cheat, judge, distress, or tempt them. We try not to persecute them or even ignore them. We are ready and eager to commit ourselves to a life of service in behalf of others. We are ready to meet whatever requirements are demanded by our errand before the Lord.

We give freely of our means, our time, and our energies to further the kingdom of God. Oh, what miracles a change in values brings as we come to this point of commitment to the gospel of Jesus Christ!

The end result of this process of conversion, growth, and change is being born again, or becoming spiritually Christ's children. The person who is so awakened is strengthened in his efforts to quit smoking, to keep the Sabbath, or to be more loving to his mate and his children.

Resisting old habits is a struggle, but in the resisting, one sees the fruits of such a personal change. The resulting state of faith leads to the next step until eventually the desire to sin leaves altogether. We don't merely resist any longer. The desire to sin is swept away in the wake of conversion to new values. This is usually believable only to those who have actually experienced it. That is why the Lord tells us to experiment upon the word and find out for ourselves. (See Alma 32:27 and Moroni 10.)

President N. Eldon Tanner tells the story of his young grandson who learned the powerful lesson and ultimate joy of self-mastery with an appropriate value system. He visited with this little grandson when he was a deacon and had completed 100 percent attendance at all meetings his first year. President Tanner was justifiably proud of the young man and said to him, "If you'll continue in this pattern until you are old enough to go on a mission, I'll finance it." The boy persisted in perfect attendance. On one occasion, he had an opportunity to go on a weekend trip to an island where church attendance was impossible. It was exciting to contemplate such a time with cousins and an uncle, the sort of experience a boy would relish. But on his own, remembering his goal and commitment, he determined to stay home rather than miss church and spoil his record.

Another time, the young man broke his leg and, as the doctor was attending him, the first thing the boy said to him was, "Doctor, will I be able to go to church tomorrow?" And he did—on crutches! One who is less committed might have valued a chance to stay home and watch television.

When the young man turned nineteen, he came to his grandfather Tanner and said, "Grandpa, I have been 100 percent ever since we made our deal. Are you ready to uphold your end of the agreement?" It was a proud grandfather who set up the financial aid for that young man's mission, for he not only had his values squarely in place, but the fruits of his chosen lifestyle had prepared him impressively for his mission.

This is the story of a remarkable young person. However, converts of all ages change their values when they put aside the things of the world to join the Church and accept its strong personal disciplines. The boy's life isn't over when he goes on a mission. He, like the new Church member, has higher levels to climb to as he grows in the gospel. This is true of each one of us, whatever our age and whatever our stage of spiritual growth.

The scriptures teach us that where our treasure is, there our heart will be also. (Matthew 6:21.) The Lord counseled his disciples not to lay up treasures upon earth, where moth and rust will corrupt and where thieves can break through and steal, but to lay up treasures in heaven. To get a new value system is a blessing with eternal ramifications and as fine a thing as we can do for ourself.

Alma asked his people if they had experienced the mighty change in their hearts—the change that had made their fathers such happy people. Then he gave the following specific questions to help them in their personal assessment. They are a good guide for us, as well, as we evaluate our values.

1. Have we experienced a change of heart—maybe not the classical "mighty change," but a shift from former thinking?

2. Do we exercise faith in the redemption of Him who created us?

3. Do we look forward with an eye of faith, to stand before God to be judged according to the deeds that have been done in the mortal body?

4. Can we imagine ourselves hearing the voice of God?

5. Can we look up to God at that day with pure hearts and clean hands?

6. Have we received his image in our countenances?

7. Do we think of being saved?

8. Have we ever felt moved upon by redeeming love? Do we feel so now?

9. Have we kept ourselves blameless before God?

10. Could we say, if called forth at this time, that we have been sufficiently humble?

11. Are we stripped of pride?

12. Are we stripped of envy?

13. Do we mock others or heap persecution of any kind upon them?

14. Of what fold are we? In whose camp are we? On what side are we? Who is our master, our king?

15. Do we persist in wearing costly apparel and setting our hearts upon the vain things of the world, upon our riches?

16. Do we suppose we are better than others?

17. Do we turn our backs upon the poor and the needy, and withhold our substance from them?

18. Do we understand that no matter how we answer, what we say, the word of God must be fulfilled anyway?

Consider this definition of value: worth in usefulness or importance to the possessor; utility or merit. Value also means precious, beyond price, important, significant, superior, to prize, to esteem.

What then should we value? What will be of most worth to

us? What does the Lord deem valuable? What are we willing to do to preserve these values?

C. S. Lewis said that if there were no life after death, it wouldn't matter much if a man became crotchety and unpleasant in his old age, treating people as poorly as he felt inclined. But if there were life after death, it would certainly matter how a man grew old!

And it matters what a man values, what treasures he stores up in his heart, what master he serves, and what model he follows. It matters what information he acts upon. His eternal life depends upon it.

One of the great spiritual moments in scriptural history comes following King Benjamin's magnificent rendering of gospel truths, when the people were so inspired and motivated that they all cried with one voice, "Yea, we believe all the words which thou hast spoken unto us; and also, we know of their surety and truth, because of the Spirit of the Lord Omnipotent, which has wrought a mighty change in us, or in our hearts, that we have no more disposition to do evil, but to do good continually." (Mosiah 5:2.) Their values had changed.

All scriptures or ideas that provoke a change in attitude affect our values. The Lord gave a system for man to make his decisions by:

"For behold, the Spirit of Christ is given to every man, that he may know good from evil; wherefore, I show unto you the way to judge; for every thing which inviteth to do good, and to persuade to believe in Christ, is sent forth by the power and gift of Christ; wherefore ye may know with a perfect knowledge it is of God." (Moroni 7:16.)

This should become our value system for our lives as well as the lives of others. In almost all scriptural material we are given helps for our value system. A great example is the sermon of the Savior in the Book of Mormon:

"Yea, blessed are the poor in spirit who come unto me, for theirs is the kingdom of heaven.

"And again, blessed are all they that mourn, for they shall be comforted.

"And blessed are the meek, for they shall inherit the earth.

"And blessed are all they who do hunger and thirst after righteousness, for they shall be filled with the Holy Ghost.

"And blessed are the merciful, for they shall obtain mercy.

"And blessed are all the pure in heart, for they shall see God.

"And blessed are all the peacemakers, for they shall be called the children of God.

"And blessed are all they who are persecuted for my name's sake, for theirs is the kingdom of heaven.

"And blessed are ye when men shall revile you and persecute, and shall say all manner of evil against you falsely, for my sake;

"For ye shall have great joy and be exceeding glad, for great shall be your reward in heaven; for so persecuted they the prophets who were before you." (3 Nephi 12:3-12.)

The Beatitudes are the celestial value standard for everyone who values happiness.

We can begin our ascent heavenward only by determining the rules by which we live, the point beyond which we will not step in a time of crisis or temptation, and the principles that motivate us. Such self-examination, with the gospel of Jesus Christ as our standard and gauge, can reveal to us if we are living by eternal values or if we are living merely the precepts of men, family traditions, or habits. Of course, we should be living by God's will for us. His values should be our values; then we become committed to living the gospel of Jesus Christ.

STEP SIX:
MAKING OUR COMMITMENT

A missionary stood to say farewell to his fellow workers in the gospel as he prepared to leave the mission field after his time of service. He was older by some years than the other missionaries. He was stooped slightly, and his face was lined with evidence of much physical suffering. For the first time, the others learned of his difficult life during the years of World War II. He had served in the Pacific theater of operations and had been forced to participate in the infamous march of Bataan. He had suffered a long period in a concentration camp. Because of these dreadful experiences of war he had come to hate the Japanese people mightily.

After the war, his life took a turn for the better. Eventually he answered a call to fill a mission for The Church of Jesus Christ of Latter-day Saints. Almost ironically, he was assigned to labor among the Japanese people.

It was a difficult challenge for him to go to Japan. He prayed constantly for help because his need was so great. He struggled to overcome his feelings and to find ways to effectively teach the

Japanese people the fullness of the word of God. As he prayed and served, a miraculous change occurred in his heart. He came to love those whom he had once hated. He loved them so deeply that he wept as he spoke of leaving them to go home. He bore fervent witness of the joy found in becoming fully converted to Christ. Tears spilled over his cheeks and the tears of others matched his own as he counseled everyone to follow Christ and to come to love their enemies as well as their friends.

This is the thrilling experience of one who tries to live the gospel. A small effort brings a large reward. To find a more wholesomely satisfying direction in life is the beginning of the conversion process. A knock at the door of Him who has all the answers to life and eternity is a move that brings Heavenly Father running to meet us. We all are prodigals, and we have but to turn homeward where the sure counsel is, to be welcomed. The Lord is waiting to be gracious to us, but he will force his presence upon no one.

The mighty change of heart won't come if we are among that certain type of people who are merely convinced God lives and who continue to live in the ordinary ways of the world. We must completely surrender our inner and outer life to God. President David O. McKay spoke often of the fact that the spirit is to the body what Christ is to the spirit. We know that in death the spirit leaves the body lifeless. When we choose to weaken the influence of God in our lives, our spirituality languishes proportionately. But when we draw ever closer to God, we feel more alive than under any other circumstances. It is a transforming, lightening, and uplifting process. It is often visible to others who see us grow. There is accompanying power to cope with life's demands, to stand firm in integrity, and to react in positive sweetness, love, and increased wisdom. Serenity is outer evidence of inner faith and conversion unto Christ.

To say "Thy will be done, Father, not mine" is the ultimate statement of commitment. It is at once binding and freeing. It is binding because we have declared ourselves obedient to the Lord. It is freeing because the Lord's will for us is the wisest, finest thing that could happen to us.

What, then, does it mean to be converted? Does it require more of us than the act of baptism or the statement of "Thy will be done"? In the deepest context of the gospel, to become converted means a real transformation from being a natural man to being one who yields to the enticings of the Holy Spirit. We change so that things incompatible with the gospel of Jesus Christ are unappealing and are avoided in our life. The Spirit of Christ permeates the being of one who has submitted to baptism and has covenanted to take upon himself the lifestyle of the Savior.

One of our problems seems to be complacency. Some believe that life-long membership or generations of membership in the Church assures us of a place in the celestial kingdom. Sometimes we expect that activity in church organizations marks us as devoted members. This may be true. But being devoted members of an organization and being converted to Christ are not one and the same. One is being supportive of an important effort, and the other is experiencing a literal transformation of being. The person who is so changed *knows* it, as he knows he lives. He feels it through the power of the Holy Ghost.

Each of us needs to take the giant step forward from being a believer to being one who has undergone the remarkable transformation of spirit. This is the way a heart is healed. This is the way one becomes filled at last with joy and peace.

The literal meaning of the word *convert,* according to the *American Heritage Dictionary,* is to undergo a change, to turn around, to transform. That implies more than just a gesture. It is the casting off of old beliefs and behaviors and insisting upon a different performance and attitude. One can be intellectually convinced God lives without being emotionally converted.

As the term is used in the scriptures, to become converted means to do more than mentally accept Jesus and his teachings as valid. It is to be so full of sweeping faith that one is motivated to good works. One's understanding of life's meaning, allegiance to the Church, and love of God are enriched beyond description.

One may become committed to Christ through the steps we've discussed in preceding chapters, but true conversion seems to come when we have finally reached that moment of being so changed in the way we feel about things deep within us that we repent and ask God for forgiveness. With his blessing we can become different beings.

Rebellious people can become receptive people and receptive people can become righteous people. The love of God becomes so great that such a person has a fixed determination to keep all of the Lord's commandments instead of following old patterns and values.

President Harold B. Lee once said, "Now I want to impress this upon you. . . . 'That person is not truly converted until he sees the power of God resting upon the leaders of this church, and until it goes down into his heart like fire.' Until the members of this church have that conviction that they are being led in the right way, and they have a conviction that these men of God are men who are inspired and have been properly appointed by the hand of God, they are not truly converted." (*Ensign*, July 1972, p. 103.)

On another occasion, President Lee said:

"To settle an apparent controversy among his disciples as to who would be the greatest in the kingdom of God, [Christ] said: '. . . except ye be converted, and become as little children, ye shall not enter into the kingdom of [God].' (Matthew 18:3.)

"To become converted, according to the scriptures, meant having a change of heart and the moral character of a person turned from the controlled power of sin into a righteous life. It meant to 'wait patiently on the Lord' until one's prayers can be answered and until his heart, as Cyprian, a defender of the faith in the Apostolic Period, testified, and I quote, 'Into my heart, purified of all sin, there entered a light which came from on high, and then suddenly and in a marvelous manner, I saw certainty succeed doubt.'

"Conversion must mean more than just being a 'card carrying' member of the Church with a tithing receipt, a membership card, a temple recommend, etc. It means to overcome the tendencies to criticize and to strive continually to improve inward weaknesses and not merely the outward appearances." (*Ensign*, June 1971, p. 8.)

Alma emphasized that all men must be converted, be born of the Spirit, and be changed to a state of righteousness. He added, "And thus they become new creatures; and unless they do this, they can in nowise inherit the kingdom of God." (Mosiah 27:26.)

King Benjamin counseled:

"Believe in God; believe that he is, and that he created all things, both in heaven and in earth; believe that he has all wisdom, and all power, both in heaven and in earth; believe that man doth not comprehend all the things which the Lord can comprehend.

"And again, believe that ye must repent of your sins and forsake them, and humble yourselves before God; and ask in sincerity of heart that he would forgive you; and now, if you believe all these things see that ye do them.

"And again I say unto you as I have said before, that as ye have come to the knowledge of the glory of God, or if ye have known of his goodness and have tasted of his love, and have received a remission of your sins, which causeth such exceeding great joy in your souls, even so I would that ye should remember, and always retain in remembrance, the greatness of God, and your own nothingness, and his goodness and long-suffering towards you, unworthy creatures, and humble yourselves even in the depths of humility, calling on the name of the Lord daily, and standing steadfastly in the faith of that which is to come." (Mosiah 4:9-11.)

It seems clear from the scriptures and the counsel of the prophets that in all progressive efforts to become converted, we must study with prayer and faith; we must fast and reach out for closeness with God; we must keep our mind single to God; we must keep our covenants; we must sustain authority and heed the word of the Lord as our inspired leaders give it to us; we must continually repent of small things, as well as big ones, so that we will be comfortable before God and have a quiet conscience; we must open our hearts in charity toward others with the pure love of Christ. Finally, we must be valiant, endure to the end, and contribute always to the building of the kingdom of God.

Our challenge, then, is to repent "and be converted, that [our] sins may be blotted out, when the times of refreshing shall come from the presence of the Lord." (Acts 3:19.)

How does one know when he is converted? The sequence moves along something like this: A person hears the gospel. If he is seeking truth, he prays to Heavenly Father for a witness as to the truthfulness of what he has heard. Then the Holy Spirit warms his heart or gives him some kind of witness that it is true. This is a testimony.

If this is important to him and if the feeling is strong enough, the person will repent and begin obeying God's commandments. By this, he is forgiven by God. Conversion is the result of or reward for repentance and obedience. It is not only that guilt slips away and newness of life takes its place, but the person now converted finds himself filled with Christ's love and quickly develops a feeling of complete dedication to a life after Christ.

Consider the following references from the scriptures as further enlightenment:

". . . the Spirit of the Lord came upon them, and they were filled with joy, having received a remission of their sins, and have peace of conscience, because of the exceeding faith which they had in Jesus Christ. . ." (Mosiah 4:3.)

". . . as I was thus racked with torment, while I was harrowed up by the memory of my many sins, behold, I remembered also to have heard my father prophesy unto the people concerning the coming of one Jesus Christ, a Son of God, to atone for the sins of the world.

"Now, as my mind caught hold upon this thought, I cried within my heart: O Jesus, thou Son of God, have mercy on me, who am in the gall of bitterness, and am encircled about by the everlasting chains of death.

". . . when I thought this, I could remember my pains no more; yea, I was harrowed up by the memory of my sins no more.

"And oh, what joy, and what marvelous light I did behold; yea, my soul was filled with joy as exceeding as was my pain!

". . . there could be nothing so exquisite and so bitter as were my pains. Yea, and again I say unto you, my son, that on the other hand, there can be nothing so exquisite and sweet as was my joy." (Alma 36:17-21.)

". . . the words which I had often heard my father speak concerning eternal life, and the joy of the saints, sunk deep into my heart.

"And my soul hungered; and I kneeled down before my Maker, and I cried unto him in mighty prayer and supplication for mine own soul; and all the day long did I cry unto him; yea, and when the night came I did still raise my voice high that it reached the heavens.

"And there came a voice unto me, saying: Enos, thy sins are forgiven thee, and thou shalt be blessed. And I, Enos, knew that God could not lie; wherefore, my guilt was swept away.

"And I said: Lord, how is it done?

"And he said unto me: Because of thy faith in Christ, whom thou has never before heard nor seen . . . wherefore, go to, thy faith hath made thee whole." (Enos 3-8.)

We live in a world of imperfections. There are no perfect people among us. Surely, then, there is a need for increased love and charity for each other. But we have a right to expect there will be improvement, repentance, and a constant striving toward perfection. "Wherefore, continue in patience until ye are perfected." (D&C 67:13.)

All of us must experience the mighty change in order to reach our final perfection. As well as having our own unshakable testimony of the divinity of Christ and the truthfulness of his church on earth, we should absolutely commit ourselves to following his will. He has told us what to do to have a successful experience in his plan of life for us. As we daily strive to do what he has said, we will see that he is right.

We live as faithfully as we can and the Lord blesses us with a changed heart; his Spirit fills us. The apostles in Joseph Smith's time were promised that if they were true and faithful, they would yet "be converted." To be in such positions of leadership, they must have had testimonies. Yet they were promised conversion! Remember what the Lord said to Peter: "When thou art converted, strengthen thy brethren." (Luke 22:32.) Peter was a fine man and a good teacher before he was converted. Later, the Holy Ghost descended upon the disciples of Christ like tongues of fire during the miracle at Pentecost after the Savior's death. It was then that Peter became a new man. He could speak with power from God, through the Holy Ghost, in a way that moved men. He could perform miracles in God's name. His understanding and vision increased, and he was even able to explain the happening of Pentecost, which had mystified the multitude.

Isn't this a clue to our own effectiveness as missionaries, as parents, and as servants in the system of the Church? We can help strengthen others as we become on fire about the gospel. We catch fire as we commit ourselves to do the Lord's will and experience the mighty change of heart.

We can magnify the name of Jesus Christ when we close our prayers. We should remember this isn't just a manner of speaking or a form of prayer. It should be a commitment made by us who have taken Christ's name upon us. Even the "Amen" we utter at the end of prayer can be a declaration of our determination as followers, friends, and disciples of Christ.

We can put our arms to the square in sustaining our leaders with an attitude of commitment to support, be loyal, and strive to follow well those who have been called to serve over us.

We can make a commitment as we renew all our covenants while taking the sacrament.

But what about the less obvious ways we show commitment? Are we prepared to be fully committed to expressing love to our families, acting in faith in all things, living by the Spirit, keeping all the commandments, sharing the gospel, securing our personal histories and genealogies, living in the world but being not of it?

Such a commitment is part of our covenant with God. It will reap for us great blessings. King Benjamin said this to his people when they had repented following his powerful address: "And now, because of the covenant which ye have made ye shall be called the children of Christ, his sons, and his daughters; for behold, this day he hath spiritually begotten you; for ye say that your hearts are changed through faith on his name; therefore, ye are born of him and have become his sons and his daughters." (Mosiah 5:7.)

WHEN WE ARE CONVERTED

The sweet joy of conversion and the accompanying testimony and feeling of being born again give us a newness of life. We become different. An awareness of the power of Christ's redeeming love makes us new creatures, sons and daughters of Jesus Christ who are totally converted.

With conversion comes responsibility. There are several scriptures that describe the responsibility of the converted soul. The Lord said, "And when thou are converted, strengthen thy brethren." (Luke 22:32.) Alma said, ". . . this is my glory, that perhaps I may be an instrument in the hands of God to bring some soul to repentance; and this is my joy." (Alma 29:9-10.) When the sons of Mosiah were converted, they couldn't bear that any human soul should perish; even the thought caused them to quake and tremble. (Mosiah 28:3.) Enos's first concern was for the welfare of his brethren and the Lamanites. One can see the results through the lives of converted souls. They all wanted to help their brothers and sisters in the gospel come closer to the Savior.

If the purpose of life is to come to know God the Father and his Son, Jesus Christ, and his kingdom on earth, then should we not change enough to become instruments in their hands in strengthening our brethren? Should we not consider our lives and worthiness as the kind of people that the Lord needs to teach his children? Should we not concentrate our efforts on becoming prepared teachers?

"And also trust no one to be your teacher nor your minister, except he be a man of God, walking in his ways and keeping his commandments." (Mosiah 23:14.)

A prepared teacher is one who knows God and teaches by the Spirit. "And a portion of that Spirit dwelleth in me, which giveth me knowledge, and also power according to my faith and desires which are in God." (Alma 18:35.)

A prepared teacher has the faith that through God's help he will be able to do a proper job and fulfill his responsibilities in a way that is pleasing to the Lord. (Alma 32:21-28.)

A prepared teacher follows the Lord's example. He learns how to teach as the Lord teaches: through love, through chastening, through blessing, and through teaching correct principles that his students can apply in their lives. He helps us grow through our experiences and mistakes until we gain lasting happiness.

How can each of us prepare ourselves to be teachers in the Lord's kingdom, to be the kinds of people the Lord wants in teaching positions? To achieve this goal, we must do the following:

1. *We must strengthen our faith in the Lord Jesus Christ.*

"Now faith is the substance of things hoped for, the evidence of things not seen," declared the apostle Paul. (Hebrews 11:1.) Faith is that which causes action. According to the Prophet Joseph Smith, it is the source of all intelligence in human beings. It is "the principle of action and of power." (Joseph Smith, *Lectures on Faith*, p. 61.) To strengthen our faith, we might do as Alma suggests—experiment upon the word and plant the seed. (Alma 32:26.) Paul pointed out that "faith cometh by hearing, and hearing by the word of God." (Romans 10:17.) With faith in Jesus Christ, we are able to act, using faith's power, for the benefit of those whom we teach. Without faith, we have been told, it is impossible to please God.

2. *We must try to keep ourselves spiritually in tune with the Lord.*

"And the Spirit shall be given unto you by the prayer of faith; and if ye receive not the Spirit ye shall not teach." (D&C 42:14.) When we are spiritually in tune, we are able to teach effectively. Being spiritually in tune includes loving God, listening to him, living worthy to receive his Spirit, and developing a testimony. We cannot be good teachers until we know God's will and strive to do it. With a broken heart and contrite spirit, we must be guided and directed by his will. This often means sacrificing earthly possessions and pleasures and putting God and his ways and commandments first in our lives.

3. *We must become mindful of fasting and prayer.*

"But this is not all; they had given themselves to much prayer, and fasting; therefore they had the spirit of prophecy, and the spirit of revelation, and when they taught, they taught with power and authority of God." (Alma 17:3.)

"For if ye would hearken unto the Spirit which teacheth a man to pray ye would know that ye must pray; for the evil spirit teacheth not a man to pray, but teacheth him that he must not pray. But behold, I say unto you that ye must pray always, and not faint; that ye must not perform any thing unto the Lord save in the first place ye shall pray unto the Father in the name of Christ, that he will consecrate thy performance unto thee, that thy performance may be for the welfare of thy soul." (2 Nephi 32:8-9.)

The knowledge of these two scriptures can unleash the power of fasting and prayer as we teach the word of God.

4. *We must study the scriptures.*

"Search the scriptures; for in them ye think ye have eternal life: and they are they which testify of me." (John 5:39.) The scriptures can help teach all the different aspects of preparing ourselves to teach and to serve Heavenly Father. We must study them. We must search them for answers to our questions. We must become as the sons of Mosiah: ". . . and they had waxed strong in the knowledge of the truth; for they were men of a sound understanding and they had searched the scriptures diligently, that they might know the word of God." (Alma 17:2.)

5. *We must come to know who we are.*

"The Spirit itself beareth witness with our spirit, that we are the children of God." (Romans 8:16.) Not only will we learn that we are children of God, but we will also learn that God loves us and is willing to help us any time we ask in faith. The Lord said, "Ask, and it shall be given you; seek, and ye shall find; knock, and it shall be opened unto you: For every one that asketh receiveth; and he that seeketh findeth; and to him that knocketh it shall be opened." (Matthew 7:7-8.)

6. *We must make an effort to love others.*

Jesus said, "This is my commandment, That ye love one another, as I have loved you." (John 15:12.) Are we willing to serve our brothers and sisters as our Savior has served us? Do we have that ultimate concern which brings about righteous service for others? Giving and showing love means giving time and effort, not just having a feeling. Becoming aware of others' needs will give us empathy and a better understanding of how to serve our fellowman.

7. *We must strive to have pure motives for teaching.*

We must make sure our intentions are to serve God and not to achieve personal glory. "Let your light so shine before men, that they may see your good works, and glorify your Father which is in heaven." (Matthew 5:16.)

8. *We must start the conversion process now.*

"But I have prayed for thee, that thy faith fail not: and when thou art converted, strengthen thy brethren." (Luke 22:32.) In other words, we have a responsibility to strengthen our brethren as we become converted to Jesus Christ.

Once we ourselves are prepared, we can apply the six principles of change in helping others to change.

As we come to know and respect God, those whom we teach will come to respect us. They will be far more likely to believe and follow us if we show that we are truly credible, caring, unpretentious, and trustworthy; if we are good examples; and above all, if our motives are pure.

How can we gain this respect so as to be more effective in touching the lives of our brothers and sisters?

We can let them know we truly love them. If we build special relationships with those whom we teach by spending time with them, showing them acts of kindness, and getting to know them, then we will care and they will know we care. Through our showing our love, we can create a bond of respect with them, and our power in their lives will be increased.

We can live the standards we teach. A classic example of hypocrisy is the television commercial in which a father is smoking but is, at the same time, telling his son, "Now don't you smoke." It is so difficult to gain respect when we don't do what we tell others to do. As much as some inactive parents preach to their children about church, percentages of attendance still show that inactive children generally come from inactive homes. If we want our children to live high standards, we must live them ourselves. If we want people to listen to the word of God, we must be sure the word of God is our standard of behavior.

We must be humble. Nothing detracts from a person's character more than a self-sufficient, holier-than-thou, I-can-do-anything-by-myself attitude. True humility brings respect. Growing people are at different levels of faith. We all need to lean on the Lord. (See Alma 26:12.)

We can develop skills for serving more effectively. Knowledge and skill bring power, credibility, and information that can help others. Our reputation precedes us. The great example of the Master was evident in every situation. Never was he lacking. We should persist in readying ourselves to be worthy and useful servants to him.

And finally, we can respect others for what they are and for what they can become. Every child is precious before God. Each one has some special gift. We should build upon their strengths and be quick to compliment and praise them when they are deserving of our praise. If there is need for criticism or for suggestions for improvement, we should give it only after careful and prayerful consideration and when moved upon by the Holy Ghost. Even then, we should give only in love. (See D&C 121:43.)

When a person becomes aware of his own noble being and of the worth of his soul to the Lord, and when he begins to understand the plan of life and the principles of the gospel, the mighty change has begun and he finds himself wanting to help others realize their own worth.

How can we parents, teachers, leaders, and loved ones help others build their own self-esteem? We can—

1. *Give genuine praise.*

King Benjamin let his people know of their potential, how much God cared for them, and how much God would bless them. This is a good example for us to follow for building self-esteem in others. We all like to be recognized for work well done, to feel needed, to be able to achieve. If we are alert to opportunities to praise others, their lives will indeed be lifted. But the praise must be genuine.

Praise given wholeheartedly can be magic. One family tells of the plight they found themselves in when everybody received some praise during family home evening except one young boy. Suddenly the mother remembered the lad had done well in putting the breakfast dishes away. He was elated at her praise, and a slow, satisfied smile spread across his face. But that wasn't all. The next time he did the job even better!

2. *Teach the facts of our divine nature.*

We need to remind others frequently of the spark of the divine that is in each of us. Too often we neglect to use our God-given capacities because we do not understand who we really are. We suffer from self-doubt, insecurity, lack of love, and weak direction.

To mothers especially goes the precious responsibility of instilling within the hearts of their children at the earliest stages the knowledge that they are special. Each child has the promise of godliness. Each one has an earthly mission to perform. Each one needs to be taught purpose in life, appreciation of life itself, and thankfulness for awareness of his gifts and good qualities as they unfold through the years.

3. *Give responsibility.*

Where no responsibility is given, there is no growth. The title, the job, the role, whatever it is, gives rise to performance parallel to the responsibility. Likewise, our strength in the Lord increases in our lives as we are given more responsibility and come to depend more on the Lord to accomplish our tasks.

The change in children as they are given responsibility around the home is dramatic. They feel a sense of pride in what they do to make the home better. Bishops note that youths have greater concern for the chapel after they have spent a Saturday helping to clean it.

4. *Help others to have success experiences.*

Everyone needs success experiences. Success breeds success. Thoughtful, caring teachers and parents provide opportunities for these experiences. By knowing the abilities and desires of those with whom we work, we can program events or assignments within their capabilities. Then self-esteem grows and motivation enters the soul for even better goals. Short-term goals, realistic achievements with self, with others, and on teams, can be fulfilling growth experiences.

5. *Enlist peers to help us in our efforts.*

Peer approval is extremely important during the growing stages of life. A leader or parent can enlist the help of a peer to find ways to build self-esteem in a person who is temporarily suffering from a feeling of inadequacy. To be accepted by a colleague or praised by a friend can often provide the impetus for further growth, repentance, and joy in living.

6. *Give praise over and over again.*

We need to learn how to express true appreciation, how to point out strengths, and how to demonstrate love and approval. We never know which drop of water will spill the glass over, which kind deed will bind the friendship, which boost to the spirit will make another person enthusiastic about life.

How can we help others feel the need or have the desire to change? Creating in others the feeling that they need or desire to change is the task of all teachers in whatever role they have. Motivating, giving desire, and creating enthusiasm for growth and betterment are indeed the purpose of all who desire to be instruments in the hands of God.

King Benjamin, who was dependent on God in all things, let the people know of their fallen state and the importance of the goodness of God if they were obedient. Because the people were prepared to hear the word of God, a need was created in their eyes. Our problem is often with the self-sufficient, apathetic, hateful, or frustrated person, so the method of approach to create the need varies. This is why motivation is so important as we create a climate for change.

Our enthusiasm for the gospel and our application of it to life can work wonders with others. If the hearer feels the excitement of information given by a friend or teacher, he becomes more aware of his own need to change.

When someone we love changes, we should take notice of it. The reward for change is basic even with the Lord. (See D&C 130:19-21; 84:33-40; 76.) Sometimes we feel that this is a materialistic system, but the difference occurs in emphasis. Doing the right thing for the right reason is what we are after. Motive makes the difference. The reward system must be compatible with the deed. With the Lord, righteousness brings the opportunity for a more righteous state of existence.

The personal joy received from proper performance is often sufficient reward. Increased self-esteem and self-discipline can be the reward. Sometimes, however, we need to help the learner become aware of this attitude.

The Lord continually uses trials to help us realize our need for the gospel in our lives. The wise teacher points this out. When a person is in a situation that requires help, it is an ideal time for change. Teaching another person to be aware of real needs regarding eternal life, which people are often oblivious to, is vital in bringing about the mighty change. Realizing the blessings given to us by God is also vital to change.

The opportunities to overcome obstacles, the understanding of our potentialities, and the realization of what is expected of us can all be catalysts that start the process of change.

How can we give information to others that is so specific that they follow it?

Information to act upon specifically brings a more realistic change. Generalities and abstract terms make the task of change difficult. It is interesting to note that for every principle or doctrine given, the Lord gives specific ways to apply it to our lives. Preparation of the learner through prayer, fasting, studying the scriptures, pondering, being naturally motivated through a problem, and developing awareness can enhance the changing experience. Like the law of the harvest, the soil (or learner) can be prepared for the seed so that greater growth can occur.

How we explain what is to be done and how we deliver this message can make a great impact upon how it is received and acted upon by those we teach. In our delivery, we should relate the subject to the learner's level of faith and to the understanding of what he can do now. We should also set a time, a place, and a way for him to start making the change through setting goals, making plans, acting with diligence, and evaluating, replanning, and beginning again.

Most problems in interpersonal communication concerning change, especially in the relationships of parent and child, leader and follower, and teacher and student, occur because of different value systems. Everyone has a value system based on things he has heard, seen, felt, experienced, or had forced upon him. His secret desires, frustrations, or exposures in life have also had an influence on him. This is why the admonition to teach children early is so important. They need to begin to set up their own criteria of how to judge things. Moroni tells us that the way to judge all things is by whether or not they persuade men to come unto Christ. (Moroni 7:16.) This being the ideal to work toward, a progressive approach to value change is important.

How can we help others create a new value system?

Where our treasure or something we value lies, there will our heart be also. (See Luke 12:34.) In Hebrew, "heart" refers to the center of things, the inner man, the governing center, character, personality, will, the mind and spring of all desire. In other words, as a man thinketh in his heart, so is he.

In creating a new value system, it is important that the heart be broken and softened so the things of the Lord can enter, bringing about a new heart, a new treasure, a new value system based upon the Lord Jesus Christ.

A new value system can be brought about by putting into

practice the principles of change: respect, self-esteem, feeling a need, and commitment. The purpose and application of the change must be relevant to life. We must feel that the change will be productive and will bring a sense of achievement and satisfaction.

We must teach true principles and concepts that will affect attitude and character, which will in turn affect the value decisions that must be made. The blessing of change in one's life is realized through actual performance; therefore, we must create experiences that allow the person who desires to change to hear correct principles and then to act upon them.

It is important that we understand the relationship of the change to happiness. Most people value happiness as their greatest desire. Therefore, we must show the difference between momentary pleasure or pseudo-happiness and the lasting joy, true happiness, and eternal life that result from total commitment to a Christlike life.

It is also important to show the value of the change to our environment. Environment dictates how we act until our level of conversion is sufficiently developed to govern our actions. Thus parents, leaders, and teachers must create the best environment possible for those whom they lead or teach so proper value systems can be learned at an early age.

Retrospect is a great teacher when it comes to making changes in lives. Through past experiences of ourselves and others we can change and improve our value systems. A great example of this is found in the Book of Mormon in the story of the rise and fall of the Nephite nation.

Changing does require time and effort. When a person has been given an assignment that requires effort, time, and sacrifice, and has sufficient motivation and encouragement to complete that assignment, he will place great value upon his achievement. We all tend to appreciate more that which comes with real effort on our part than that which comes easily or is handed to us with no sacrifice expected.

Developing a new value system can have far-reaching

effects—it can change a person, a family, a state, a nation, even the world.

When King Benjamin finished his sermon, the people all said, "We believe." They had no more desire to sin. They entered into a covenant. They made their commitment. (Mosiah 5:2-7.) We, like King Benjamin, can help others feel this way.

How do we assist others in making the commitment?

When we bring about an opportunity for the learner to make a commitment, we should do all in our power to support and encourage him. We should recognize that he is the one who must make the decision and keep the commitment. We should reinforce him with genuine support and praise, and show that others also support the change, especially Heavenly Father. (See 1 Nephi 3:7 and Alma 26:12.) We should be a helper, not a judge.

We should demonstrate acts of faith and prayer in the learner's behalf, and show him the fruits of commitment. We should help him establish goals that are attainable, that he can commit himself to achieve.

Commitment is a by-product of self-mastery and self-discipline, and the learner needs constant support and encouragement to develop these necessary tools. He also needs specific information on how, where, and when he can achieve his commitment.

The process of commitment and covenant-making is basic to the gospel of Jesus Christ, not only as we begin to change, but also as we need reinforcement in the process of changing. Our challenge is to heed the words of the scripture: "Repent ye therefore, and be converted, that your sins may be blotted out, when the times of refreshing shall come from the presence of the Lord." (Acts 3:19.) Following the six basic principles discussed in this book can aid us in this effort.

If we are to be of the greatest value to our Heavenly Father and our fellowmen, when we are converted we must strengthen our brethren. We must learn what it takes to teach the world effectively. We must teach by example and precept to help bring about change and conversion in others.

To be an instrument in the hands of the Lord, to bring change into someone's life, is singularly rewarding. To assist others in making the change is to be Christlike, for Christ's mission was to bring to pass the immortality and eternal life of man. Our mission can parallel his if we accept our responsibility as parents, teachers, church leaders, and caring friends, to help bring about the eternal life of those who come under our influence. Living worthily so that the Holy Ghost may be our guide and revelator in this momentous task is part of the challenge.

Change in ourselves and change in others comes about through the power of the Savior and through application of his principles. One who assists in the noble work tastes real joy. Alma said, ". . . I have labored without ceasing, that I might bring souls unto repentance; that I might bring them to taste of the exceeding joy of which I did taste." (Alma 36:24.)

Now is the time to make the commitment. As President Spencer W. Kimball has said, "Do it!"

WHY NOT CHANGE?

Why not make the mighty change? The people in the City of Enoch changed. Alma changed, and so did Paul. The good people described in 4 Nephi changed. They lived ever closer to Christ and were blessed by him until they became participants in a near-perfect society. There are people among us today who conscientiously strive to treat others as they would like to be treated themselves, who strive to become peacemakers, to mourn with those who mourn, to be meek and lowly of heart but bold in defending righteousness. They love wholesomely and unselfishly. They forgive, and try to right wrongs. They do not judge, but stand as lights, crutches, or guides to the needful.

The place to start the mighty change is with ourselves. The time is to start the mighty change is now. The rewards are immediate and long-lasting. We need to change whatever is not what it ought to be or can be. If we are carrying a burden of guilt, if we have habits that are short circuiting our power, if we lack sufficient of the gospel, if we are only convinced that Christ lives but not converted to living his ways, changing can be a blessing.

One of the tender moments in the scriptures is Mormon's farewell to his son Moroni. It could be depressing if one chooses to dwell upon the grievous behavior of the Lamanites and of the people of Morianton described by Mormon in his record. In their wars against each other these tribes lost all touch with the Lord and performed many abominations. They had gone so far they could no longer be called a civilized people. Mormon said of them, "I know that they must perish except they repent and return unto him [Christ]." (Moroni 9:22.) Then Mormon wrote the pleas that echo any parent's desire for the children he loves and for whom he wants the best:

"My son, be faithful in Christ; and may not the things which I have written grieve thee, to weigh thee down unto death; but may Christ lift thee up, and may his sufferings and death, and the showing of his body unto our fathers, and his mercy and long suffering, and the hope of his glory and of eternal life, rest in your mind forever.

"And may the grace of God the Father, whose throne is high in the heavens, and our Lord Jesus Christ, who sitteth on the right hand of his power, until all things shall become subject unto him, be, and abide with you forever." (Moroni 9:25-26.)

This counsel applies to the discussion in this book, for it is not intended to weigh the reader down with tedious reminders of familiar commandments, personal imperfections, or the long and hard road to eternal life. Rather, it is intended to remind the reader that the gospel is a message of hope and joy with irrevocably declared laws that bring beautiful blessings when they are abided.

When we look at the promises for righteous living and at the protection from the anguish of evil provided if we keep the word of the Lord, we should feel lifted up. When we think of Christ, his mission, his love, and his blessings for us, how full our hearts should be!

Moroni himself gives us the clue to all of this. His own farewell to mankind before he sealed up the records and hid them away centuries before Joseph Smith received them is beautifully relevant and motivating. It seems highly appropriate that this book should end as the Book of Mormon ends—with the challenge to change:

"Yea, come unto Christ, and be perfected in him, and deny yourselves of all ungodliness; and if ye shall deny yourselves of all ungodliness and love God with all your might, mind and strength, then is his grace sufficient for you, that by his grace ye may be perfect in Christ." (Moroni 10:32.)

INDEX

WITHDRAWN

JUN 2 5 2024

DAVID O. McKAY LIBRARY
BYU-IDAHO